From Fear to Freedom: My Journey

3 Steps to Overcome Your Past
and Find Freedom

Hena Husain

Table of Contents

Disclaimer

Acknowledgments

Forward

Introduction

How to Use This Book

STEP ONE - REINVENT

Chapter 1: How Did I Get So Afraid? ...19

Chapter 2: How Does Fear Affect Your Relationships? ...36

Chapter 3: How Does Judgment Hurt Us? ...49

Chapter 4: How and Why Do We Self Sabotage? ...60

STEP TWO - REPROGRAM

Chapter 5: Why Is Dealing With Stress Important? ...75

Chapter 6: How Can We Overcome Our Fears? ...83

Chapter 7: What Is the Role of Energy? ...100

Chapter 8: Is There Freedom In Forgiveness? ...115

STEP THREE - REINFORCE

Chapter 9: Is Love the Answer? ...123

Chapter 10: Being of Service ...142

Afterword

Recommended Resources

Disclaimer

This book is a tool to help you heal yourself. It is not designed to diagnose, prevent, or treat any medical condition. Every effort has been made to ensure that the book is as accurate as possible. Since we are self-publishing to stay accessible, please email mistakes you find for continued improvement: **Balance4Life.1@gmail.com**.

The processes used in this book are not intended to replace professional mental health counseling in any way. Any claims made in this book are individual in nature, and no guarantees are made.

owledgements

I would like to thank my husband, Nasir. Without his encouragement, I could not have written a book on such a highly sensitive topic. My three kids Meher, Abbas, and Akbar — my three pillars of support. Thank you to Ellen Waara for all your guidance in getting the book written. Also Wayne Dyer, the self-transformation giants who came before me, as well as the insight from my clients. Thank you for all of your support in getting this book published.

Thank you,

Hena

FOREWORD

Hena Husain has written a brave, bold, and beautiful book about the traumatic experiences in her earlier life, her recollection of these in her adult life, and her quest to heal herself.

She shares with us her painful experiences of being molested (in different ways, to different degrees, at different times in her life, by different males). These experiences occurred within the context of an intact nuclear family, and a loving extended family. Her account reminds us of the necessity of conveying to our children, through words and deeds, that there is nothing they could tell us that we wouldn't want to hear. It is conviction in a child's mind that usually allows him or her to share unpleasant, scary, and shameful experiences with a parent, safe in the knowledge that they will be heard without being doubted, accused, blamed, or being told that it must be their fault.

When there is disbelief on the part of the parent this then becomes an additional trauma, superimposed on the primary one, as the child's sense of safety and expectation of being looked after and protected is shattered again. The child's best defense under such circumstances is knowledge (to be forewarned is to be forearmed) that in such a situation, what is happening is *never* their fault and they have a right to scream for help.

if, despite all precautions, a child's body or mind (through its and efforts to intimidate) are abused, the next important step is for the child to be able to quickly tell a trusted adult so that she can be protected and helped and the predator called to justice. Hena describes, like many children, not being able to do so. And nobody asked. Nor was anybody curious or suspicious. Thus, the first set of traumatic experiences laid down painful scar tissue in her psyche, as though she was to blame for what happened.

Hena has realized over time that in addition to sexual molestation, death, loss, and separations have played a major role in living a fearful life. These experiences added to her sense of anxiety and her worry about the fragility of life. At the same time, her sense of her father as strong and loving, and the sustenance she experienced from her extended family, also comes through. Human beings and their lives are highly complex and multilayered. Hena's is no exception. She allows us to experience all the layers, discreetly and with subtlety, but with complete honesty.

It was while training to become a Clinical Hypnotherapist that she became clearly aware of feelings and memories surrounding her abuse. She started allowing herself to feel the locked up, compartmentalized parts of herself, tucked away for so long. She used various well-researched and established modalities in her own healing process. She explains her three-step process which she uses with all her clients to help them overcome trivial or traumatic past experiences. It is a road map to recovery and finding freedom.

May we all find the wisdom to understand that what we are trying to find outside ourselves is but an illusion, and that if only we could discover healing within our own selves, we would easily lead lives of great contentment and be able to be at peace with who we really are.

Deepest congratulations to Hena Husain on writing this much-needed book.

Aisha Abbasi, M.D. Psychoanalyst/Psychiatrist
Author of *The Rupture of Serenity: External Intrusions and Psychoanalytic Technique*

Introduction

- Oprah Winfrey

I don't want to tell this story. My breath catches as I picture you reading this, fifty years after it happened, even though I know it wasn't my fault. How could it take me this long to find my voice? Until now, I could tell no one. Please forgive me.

My story may seem irrelevant, but stories can profoundly affect us and we may not even be aware of their hold on us. When we rewrite our own stories, the world around us shifts. It only took me a moment to decide to be silent, but it took me the rest of my life to uncover the layers of pain and fear I hid beneath.

Some people may wish I had remained silent. But I have grown to the point where it is no longer my secret to keep. I ask the Divine for the courage to speak to you now so that we all can heal. Our culture, race, religion, or sexual orientation doesn't matter. We are all connected. It's my responsibility to heal myself so that I can serve humanity.

The time is now.

Please take my hand and walk with me. As the tears fall, hearts open and heal. It is worth the walk through my past from *Fear to Freedom*. As I dragged my burdens and secrets through life alone, I learned slowly that these problems are universal. I discovered that there are tools and resources to help. I offer these to you with love so that you can free yourself from fear and enter your rightful bliss of love and freedom.

I'm not sure which tool will heal the void in your heart, but I know that each one has worked for me in a unique and powerful way. I found that silently suffering alone kept me stuck in the past. Once you change your mind, you change your life.

It's time to let go.

It's time to begin.

Join me as we share a journey from fear to freedom, where questions become a quest and unexpected answers are revealed. I shared my knowledge and experience to help my readers overcome their past in their own minds.

This book is an introduction to a three-step process that helped me overcome my fears and find freedom to live a life of purpose and fulfillment.

I believe it is my purpose to empower my readers through the questions that become my quest. Life is about exploring the questions and there are no right or wrong answers, just possibilities.

Consider the possibility: What would you do if you knew you could not fail?

One day happiness arrived and I realized that I had conquered all my demons, but that I was standing in a clearing and felt more like a princess of serendipity than a victim. I looked over my shoulder and could see mountains of fears I had climbed and moved beyond.

I decided that my story had merit for others that are travelling this way. I share it in the spirit of adventure. We are all human beings becoming enlightened by our near brushes with the dragons along the way.

The fire breathing dragons were fears I had to face inside. I was afraid to speak up, and that dis-ease was showing up through weight gain and diabetes. I was afraid of being judged, so I stuffed my feelings and put on a great act to make sure that I looked good. I was afraid of not being loved, so I shut down and didn't share my real self with my mom, my husband, or anyone else.

I was a basket case inside. I was overcompensating for my not-good-enough program by being the school prefect, constantly studying, throwing perfect parties, and working ceaselessly to be perfect enough to receive the love I needed.

I used to be so afraid of being alone that I couldn't go to the bathroom or go to sleep alone. It delayed my career as a hypnotherapist, because I was terrified that I couldn't travel to any of my certification seminars, or sleep through the night when I finally arrived.

Along the way, I began to listen to myself while I wrote out my angers and fears. Journaling became problem solving, and instantly released some of the energy and layers covering my inner glory. It took a long time for me to see glory instead of gory. Once I scraped the layers away, I began to access my inner creativity and find the gifts of acceptance and bliss beneath the haze of depression and pretending.

My three-step process is simple yet profound:

- **REINVENT** – self-awareness, where you are now, your story.
- **REPROGRAM** – utilizing hypnosis, EFT, NLP, Reiki and chakra balancing.
- **REINFORCE** – taking action daily, using your tools.

My absolute favorite tool, hypnosis, has been my spiritual grace. It was the turning point for me. By finding the traumas, and going deeper into the blind spots that were hidden away, I began to be more loving and less judging.

Emotional Freedom Technique (EFT) became my anywhere instant fix tool. A few taps with that little hammer, and the monsters in my mind began to leave. It was all beginning to be a dream, and I realized that my thoughts were casting the characters and making up the scenes!

Reiki and Chakra balancing are energy work for emotional healing. It moves stuck cellular energy by aligning us with our authentic energy we came to be. Sort of like an energy body massage - nurturing and loving.

This is my quest to show you where I was when I was stuck and how I've gotten where I am today. I will show you what I do when I fall into the dead-end places and what works for the long haul versus short term gratification of quick fixes.

Let's be clear, we are here to help each other along. I have been blessed with many wise teachers, and I would never have gotten where I am without their kindness and patience. I honor their gifts as I share them with you.

My hope is that they will serve you as they have served me, and that together we will continue to heal as one sacred and deserving human family.

It does not matter where you are or if you are like me. You are unique. This route to freedom is customized and created with you in mind. You are the one who's commitment and courage will carry you through to where our common Mother, that loves us all equally and sent us forth to be victorious, is calling us home with great love and encouragement. We will learn together how to hear the inner voice of our intuitive greatness and harness our capacity for peace.

With Great Love,
Hena

How to Use This Book

People form their emotional pain in layers, like onions. This book is a resource to help take off one layer at a time. I will share my darkest moments, and how I was able to peel these layers of discomfort from myself, in the hopes that you are able to benefit from my pain and struggle. It's a patient and tender process, requiring great faith and loving support.

With each reprogramming tool, I identify what it is, how it works, and why it's important to do it. The physical act of writing reveals what you need, bringing to the surface a diagnostic message from your wise inner being. This is your safe space.

You can't change overnight. I used the resources in this book over several years. What is important is to begin and to become aware. It is in the becoming that a newer and healthier version of yourself will evolve. Awareness is the first step in reinventing yourself.

As you explore your own stories, you will you open the doors to a new self-awareness, you will realize that you take on belief systems that hold you back from a joy-filled and happy life. Together, we will find the beliefs that keep you stuck. Releasing the stuck energy from these false belief systems and limiting decisions will bring you peace and freedom. This is where you reprogram your mind.

Fear to Freedom is divided into three parts. These three parts represent my own change process and can serve as a foundation for your own healing. As you read, I will take you through my stages of **reinvention, reprogramming,** and **reinforcement**. At the end of each chapter are **action steps for healing**. You must actually stop reading and do the work if you want the benefits of healing. Please come back and do them as many times as it takes. If you find any of them particularly helpful, use them every day, as I have done. This is important to reinforce the new you.

As I reveal my story, I introduce different resources I used to get unstuck and get out of denial. If you take on too many issues at one time, it gets overwhelming. Deal with each issue and bring about closure before you move to the next.

ACTION STEP: Journaling

The method of writing which I prefer is journaling and is part of the reinforcement step. It is now well-proven that journaling can help your mental wellbeing. Find a pen and a notebook that is private, so no one will peak. Take a deep breath, then write at least two pages.

It doesn't matter what the words are. But it is essential to keep writing without stopping. If you can't think of anything, just write "I can't think of anything", until you can come up with something else. The purpose of the activity is to keep going without hesitation.

When you lose yourself in your writing, you may discover you are able to speak from a place that remembers; somewhere deep down. Sometimes I will write for two and a half pages, and in the final paragraph find a treasure. Just two pages a day can help you create your own book in a few months.

Whatever I couldn't say in person, I learned to say in my journal. After two pages the ranting would shift to peace and solutions. I released the energy, walked away and it felt good. Then I showed up as loving rather than judging with my family and friends.

STEP ONE REINVENT

Chapter 1 How Did I Get So Afraid?

My Story

"Failure is just a way for our lives to show us we're moving in the wrong direction, that we should try something different."

- Oprah Winfrey

Dacca, Bangladesh –1963

I was born in Dacca, Bangladesh in 1963. It was East Pakistan until 1971, when after a bloody civil war the country was re named Bangladesh. East Pakistani's were mostly Muslims, followed Islamic law, and ate *halal* (permissible) food within their culture.

My mom's oldest sister married my dad's oldest brother, and both of our families lived together in two houses side by side. We mingled as one unit in a chaotic, joyful blend of cousins, siblings, aunts, and uncles. A live-in housekeeper, cook, and other servants completed our home. Thirty people living in two homes with four bedrooms each. In America that seems crowded, but for us it was community; our beloved family. I had four older brothers and I was the long-awaited daughter.

When I arrived, I was adored. I had everything I needed. I was smug in my status as the only daughter in a family of generationally stacked males.

The fullness of our family, the constancy of my cousins, and the richness of the colors, smells, and textures of my days was a dream that I took for granted. I was rarely alone. My cousins were like sisters and brothers. It didn't occur to me that I should cherish the bliss of being enough; one family in love. It never occurred to me that it would suddenly shift.

Age 3 –Dacca, Bangladesh – 1966

My father was on a business trip in London when he received a telegram from Bangladesh that said: "Your daughter has died. Come home."

He took the first flight, the most distressing flight of his life, believing he had lost his only daughter for whom he'd begged, bargained with, and beseeched God for after having four sons. How would he comfort his wife and what would he say to her? What would he do?

For seven hours, he was a tormented strategist. Upon landing, he found out that there was a death, but it was my sweet three-year-old cousin, the daughter of his only brother. He was relieved and saddened when he found out that she had drowned in the bathtub. This intense moment of huge loss was accompanied by the joy that I was still alive.

I was a married adult when he first told me this story, and it brought me to tears. I was overwhelmed with his love for me. It cemented our treasured relationship. I felt so special and adored. The sparkle in my father's heart reached into my soul. It was just a few years before he died that he shared this heartfelt story with me.

Fear of Water

Because my cousin drowned, my mother developed an intense fear that it could happen to me. She became overprotective whenever I was around water. She would scream at me when we came close to water, even in parks and lakes. Mom's intense fear rooted in me too. Lacking boundaries, I didn't know it wasn't mine.

To this day, I sometimes clench up when I get near beautiful water. The deep impact of my cousin dying and my mother's reaction caused post-traumatic stress. I'm an empath, and can feel others' emotions. It's a great asset in my work and world. But as a child, I could not distinguish between my reality and other people's perceptions and emotions.

Age 5 – Dacca, Bangladesh – 1968

Fear of Death

Shortly after my cousin drowned, her older sister died suddenly at age sixteen. This second family death affected us all, but nothing was said of it. There was no explanation, and we never talked about it as a family. This was a void and an unsolved mystery in my mind.

I was five at the time, and believed that young children could die anytime. All that in a five-year-old mind gave me an intense fear of death. I wondered, who is going to die next? Will it be me? I decided that there was no such thing as forgiveness or grace for some things. I filed this fear and used it later for building the wall of my own experiences and unspeakable story. It seemed as if the ghosts between the walls whispered that I too could suddenly become nameless.

As children, some of our fears come from our own experiences, but some come from the authority figures in their lives. Mom had major fears about death due to her own insecurities, and now they became mine.

Fear of Abandonment

My parents went on a business trip to London, England. This was the first time that they left me alone with my extended family members. I felt abandoned.

It was then that I was first traumatized. Our housekeeper's thirteen-year-old son took my hand and led me from the kitchen to the bedroom.

Much later I recalled the incident in a hypnosis session:

The door opens and I enter. The smells of dahl and curry mingle in my nose and the filaments of dust seem suspended as the sunlight filters through the curtains of my childhood home. It's hot, and I'm lonely.

A boy is staring at me in a way that I don't understand. Still, he's the only one there, so I ask, "Do you want to play?"

I'm holding a toy and he takes it roughly away and pushes me back in the corner. I'm used to roughhousing and think he's just playing at first. But he pins me down and keeps me from moving while he mounts me and presses hard. It hurts, and I begin to cry.

All I can think in my five-year-old mind is, "Where is everyone? Where's my mom, my four older brothers?" I can hear them playing outside. I cry out, "Help!"

"Be quiet or I'll tell them you were bad and you'll suffer forever. Don't say anything to anybody," he hisses. I don't understand the words, yet his mean eyes hold mine, and I understand his threat. I stop protesting.

Something left me then. The voice I used for protection felt like it was stuffed with cotton and this kept me from speaking up. I was usually a provocative, playful, vivacious, pretty, and pampered child. Now, I felt alone and afraid.

Age 7 – Dacca, Bangladesh to Karachi, Pakistan – 1971

Fear of Scarcity

In 1971, tensions ignited a civil war between Pakistan, India and the indigenous people of Bangladesh; we were forced to move to West Pakistan, now just Pakistan after the separation of the East wing of that country. My dad, whom I've always called Abu, was well connected and privy to the impending danger. He warned his whole family to leave Dacca, yet my mother's brother's family chose to stay.

My parents, brothers, and I took the last flight out of Dacca airport, just before it closed. I later learned we were the last people to leave.

All of my first cousins, aunts, and uncles who remained were thrown in prison for two years. It was traumatic for us to be separated from the rest of our family. If only they had listened to Abu, they wouldn't have suffered for two years.

Moving Away

Moving from Dacca to Karachi was hard. We left it all and walked away with the clothes on our backs. Like the destruction of a fire, all of our assets and property were gone overnight. It was devastating.

My fear of death intensified during the war. I remember vividly that sirens would go off at all hours. We were rushed inside the house and hidden under the bed. My seven-year-old mind thought: "Will I have anything left after today? Is today my last day?" In case all of my possessions were destroyed in the war, I made a little plastic survival bag with small things: some coins, a match light, and some candy.

Abu's sound business acumen, money, and strong political associations with the overthrown regime put our family at great risk. We would have suffered. He had the foresight and fortitude to walk away from his money, and choose a life where his family would prosper and thrive again over time.

Abu was kind and generous to a fault. A self-made millionaire, he was disciplined in his habits and routines; embodying a constancy in eating, actions, and temperament. He had the knack of knowing what to say to whom, when and how.

My sense was that he wanted his sons to follow his professional and financial footsteps. It always surprised me when he confided his intimate thoughts and dreams to me, his youngest and only girl.

24

Moving Again From Karachi to Kuwait - 1972

Within nine months, we moved again from Karachi to Kuwait. Abu had taken a job in the Middle East to start a new banking business, and we joined him. Yet again, I left all my family, friends, toys and the familiarity of our home. My father and mother took only my brother, Nasim and I. They left my three older brothers, Saleem, Shameem, and Tasleem. in the care of aunts and uncles so they could attend college.

Fear of moving again consumed me, this time with a splintered family.

My Relationship with My Mother

The first time I had this feeling of not sharing and shutting down, I was seven years old. I went to an upscale British school in Kuwait, where we had just moved from Pakistan. It was a brand-new school, and a new day. It was such a strict school that they used to do physical check-ups at the nurse's office. When she did my physical check, she found lice in my hair, which was common in Pakistan. She sent me back home. She said you cannot come back to school until your hair is free of hair lice.

It was so embarrassing in front of all the kids. I was sobbing all the way to home, so horrified. After I returned, no one accepted me as a friend. They called me the girl with the head lice. I was so mad at my mom, "Why did you not clean my hair"?

I was so excited to make new friends that first day. Now I was kicked out of school for a week! No one talked to me, they laughed when I passed them in the hall. When I spoke to them they ran away. No one sat with me in class. They called me "Head Lice". That lasted a year; to prove to all of them that I am "good enough", I decided to be the best in the class. I became the prefect, the British version of class leader.

Finally, I made some Pakistani friends, and we socialized together. I was double promoted in that first year, I was taken out of the second grade and put into the third. That was a vote of confidence. I felt smart, like I could do anything. How many others in this class did that, I wondered proudly?

By age nine, I was physically developed and mentally bright. It is only now that I realize that emotionally I was guarded and had walled off a lot of feelings. My only coping mechanism was shutting down. But every shut down had a lot of anger and resentment in the background.

When I was the first girl in my class to get my menstrual period at age nine, Mom didn't even explain that it was a normal biological function for women. I thought for the longest time that my body had unique problems, when it's something that all developing young women go through. One of the most embarrassing moments in my life was walking around with stained clothes and all the other kids laughing at me. I decided at that moment that I didn't need anybody. I could figure out life all by myself.

I realize that this resentment toward my mom created a situation where I was not able to feel support or trust her with big issues in my life. Perhaps she had something similar happen to her when she was a girl? So, I withheld my feelings. No one was sympathetic because I was wearing a mask that hid my sadness.

Age 10 – Kuwait – Fall 1973

Trauma in Kuwait

I had an affluent upbringing, with many attendants. I was very athletic and my activities held me after school most days, when I would go home alone with our chauffeur.

My lean legs show beneath my uniform and carefully pressed blouse. My book bag strap is sweaty beneath my hand as I reach for the back door.

"No," the chauffeur says, "Miss Hena sits up front with me as a big girl should."

"No, I want to sit in back," I beg. "Please."

"No, you sit up front like a big girl," he insists. His strong hand presses firmly on my back, leaving no room for further protest.

My head is hurting, and my mouth is dry. My black school shoes scuff as he pushes me toward the front of the black limousine and opens the front passenger door.

I reluctantly slide inside, eyes downcast, already ashamed of what I know is coming.

"That's a good girl", he oozes and locks me inside.

My heart pounds; bitter bile begins to rise, yet I say nothing. Who would have listened? Who would have believed?

Perhaps this time, if I sit very still and hardly breathe, he'll forget about me. Yet, during the short fifteen-minute ride, he's pushing his hand up my thigh, under my skirt.

As he continues, I'm numb, and leave the scene in my mind, projecting my presence into the passing clouds, the leaves of the trees, and the passing scenery.

My face flushes and I bite my right cheek until I taste blood. It distracts me from the shame.

The car moves stealthily between the tree-lined streets of our upscale neighborhood, and I am delivered to our beautiful home, physically unharmed but emotionally devastated.

I get home at 3:30, and mother is resting in the heat of the afternoon. Nanny greets me as she always does: with kindness and a snack. I eat what I can, go to my room, close the door, and cry silently in my bed. Only for a moment or someone might see. I have a front to keep up, performing faultlessly.

I would not share this with anyone for the next forty-five years. Innocence fled long before it was time, and I was lucky his harmful probing stayed on the outside. Still, the scars of anxiety when left alone, anxiousness to please, and a feeling of inadequacy plagued me into my adult years. I believed I was not good enough; otherwise this would have never happened to me. The shame consumed me. What if someone found out?

Fear of Being Judged

He was never caught, because I couldn't speak of the unspeakable to my Muslim family. No one would have believed me or understood if I had told them. I had no one to share it with. I was the youngest in the family, and felt unheard anyway.

The fear of being judged consumed me. What's everyone going to think of me? It's probably my fault anyway. I went into shutdown and I never said anything. No one knew. No one took me by the hand to ask, "Has anyone touched you?" My self-esteem plummeted. I believed that if no one stood up for me, I must be worthless.

In Muslim culture, no one talks about abuse or sex. Even though it's just as common as in cultures where it is being talked about. The victims have no voice. Fear and shame overpower our logical thought process. Even though I was surrounded by love, I never felt loved.

I felt disembodied. I was trapped in a void where love and comfort didn't reach. Shame covered a nugget of hurt, like bitter chocolate cocooning a slug. I didn't talk about the drowned cousin or her sister. I never mentioned the nasty boy. As a family, we simply didn't discuss any of these things.

These shocks sunk all too easily, like heavy stones slowly erecting a protective wall around the authentic me. They were hidden deeply in my subconscious. If I had known that nothing was wrong with me, I would not have put them there. A disconnect caused by my own fears and condemnation was sapping my joy and vitality.

My little mind reasoned that when I will be good enough, the lovely feeling of freedom, love and belonging would return again. It felt like someone was withholding from me. It would take me many years to discover that the key that would unlock the kingdom of loving oneness was always right inside of me.

Because of my past and the Muslim culture, I wouldn't let anyone too close. I was always on guard and never alone with a boy. At all times, I made sure there was someone with me.

Because of my molestation experiences, I made a decision not to trust men fully. This had a huge impact on my relationship with my husband. I would jump through hoops to overcome my low self-esteem and low self-confidence. I became the Monitor, the teacher's pet, the social queen of the school. I was Miss Popular to prove to the world that I was worthwhile. On the outside I appeared shining, but dark shadows were frozen inside.

Age 16 – Moved from Kuwait to Vancouver BC – 1980

That spring, I graduated high school in Kuwait. I was only sixteen years old. My father chose Vancouver, Canada, for our higher studies, where I excelled academically.

I began my undergraduate career that fall. I was smart and immersed myself in my studies; driven to achieve and fueled by beliefs of not being good enough. With my confused reasoning, I believed that when I got it right I would receive the love that I used to feel before I built the wall whose foundation was low self-esteem. I had no idea that the love was still there or that the wall kept me from feeling it.

Religious Studies

During this time in Canada, my family remained active in our Muslim culture, as we always had. Our *molana* (priest) came to teach the *Koran* (the Muslim holy book) to my brother and me. He came in the middle of the afternoon while my mother was resting.

My brother leaves and it's now my turn to go into the room to read to the molana. I sit across the room from him.

"Come here, sit closer so I can hear you better", he says, pulling up a chair next to him. Reluctantly, I sit down. As soon as I do, he puts his hand on my thigh. It gives me the creeps; the heebie-jeebies.

While my mouth reads the verses, my body is frozen and my wiser mind asks quietly, "How can a man doing God's work do this to me?" My not-good-enough belief system whirs strongly in the background, manufacturing goofy reasoning.

I silently ask God, "Why does this keep happening to me? What am I doing wrong?"

But this time, I know that it isn't right. I have finally learned to stand up for myself. I stand up and say, "No, I'm not going to do this. I'll tell on you. This isn't right."

"Nobody is going to believe you", he threatens, implying that I am the bad girl.

I leave the room and tell my mom, "I don't want to read with the molana anymore."

"Why not?" she asks.

I just say "No." I don't explain why and I shutdown.

Open Communication is Vital

Growing up, my mother was not very expressive — physically or emotionally.

I felt that my mom had her own deep fears that kept her shut down. Our conversations took place with only a few words. I thought that if I told her the truth, it would devastate her and our relationship, pushing her even further away from me.

Open communication between parents and their children is important. Children need to feel comfortable sharing with their authority figures, especially during a traumatic experience. In general, sex and abuse are taboo subjects in Muslim culture, which automatically shuts down these necessary conversations. Kids need to feel safe to share their experiences with their authority figures openly and freely.

Many people react to abuse by not speaking out or claiming their rights for safety and kindness. Due to these experiences, my fears intensified and solidified. The fear and lack of safety compelled me to continuously feel unsafe in my environment. It got to the point that I could not even go to the bathroom by myself.

When clear communication between parents and children is missing, it can go one of two ways. Challenges can either create a bond of compassion, or a huge rift between them.

As a mother now, I know that open communication is vital between parents and children. What I lived with as a child could have been mitigated if my parents had the ability and knowledge to communicate, and hear me, and support me through the trauma.

It's very important for parents to believe in their child when they do express their experiences, so that the child does not feel it's their fault and builds confidence in the relationship.

Face Your Fears and Do It Anyway

When I moved to Vancouver I decided to find freedom in this western country in the way I perceived it at that time; I go and get my first job. My mother was totally against it saying, "Women who work outside cannot be a good wife and mother". That belief took me decades to overcome.

I wanted to prove her wrong. My brother Shamim was selling Encyclopedia Britannica and got me a job in the company. On my first day, the driver left me all alone in a subdivision an hour away from home. I was terrified. As I was pacing up and down the unfamiliar streets I cried for half an hour. I was thinking about what might happen if I knocked on one of the doors. Fear of rejection and abandonment came over me. Fear of being violated consumed me.

Finally, I asked myself, "What is the worst that can happen?" Then I knocked on the door. A beautiful young oriental family opened the door and welcomed me inside. To my surprise, they purchased the encyclopedia for $1000! That sale instantly boosted my self-confidence and self-esteem. All the previous fear momentarily left me. I realized I could do anything I set my mind to, just face the fears, and then do it anyway. I also started taking swimming lessons to overcome my fear of water. Everything started to unfold.

FEAR is **F**alse **E**vidence **A**ppearing as **R**eal. The number one fear is public speaking. People would rather be in a coffin than speak on stage. Only two things can replace fear: **knowledge** and **action**. When the desire to be free is bigger than the fear, new possibilities start to show up.

ACTION STEP: Identify Your Fears

You may not know where your fears originated, but the first step to reinvent yourself is awareness. Look over the following list and see if you identify with any of the following fears. You may also have fears that are not on this list.

Think about each fear individually.

How does this fear affect your life right now?

Do you know where it comes from?

Write it in your journal. Do not worry if you do not have all the answers; the important thing at this stage is you take time to reflect and write down your feelings, beliefs and decisions you took on as a child.

Write in your journal:

Where are your fears coming from?

What are your childhood stories?

Some Common Fears You Might Experience:

Rejection

Shameful Secrets

Not Being Good Enough

Speaking in Public

Looking Good

Failure/Success

Death/Darkness

Intimacy

Flying

Driving

Heights

Drowning

Abandonment

Socializing

Insects

Chapter 2 How Fear Affects Relationships

"Happiness is never something you get from other people. The happiness you feel is in direct proportion to the love you give."

- Oprah Winfrey

Age 16 – Karachi, Pakistan – 1979
How I Met My Husband

Just before moving from Kuwait to Vancouver for my undergraduate degree, I returned to Karachi for a wedding of my future husband's brother. He would be married in a week-long celebration.

Nasir's dad used to work with Abu. He had known me since I was five and he was eleven. As children, we would go to lunch and movies together with the uncles.

There were no sisters or females in their immediate family, since they were a family of five brothers. I took on the female role of hostess for the weeklong festivities and arrangements, as I loved to throw parties and prove myself.

During previous visits to my homeland, my long locks and wide eyes would magnetize eligible bachelors. This time, Nasir seemed to be the one infatuated with me. I enjoyed his flirtatious glances and thought it was just another crush.

Nasir was flirting and paying attention to me during the wedding. He was genuinely in love with me, yet I had no clue. During the entire wedding-week celebration, we had constant eye contact, and I enjoyed it.

He was very good looking and well mannered, which was something I liked. He was also well dressed. To me that was important, I couldn't marry anyone who wasn't well dressed. Women usually prefer marrying men who share the qualities of their father.

My father, being in the financial and banking industry, was always in a suit. Abu was the most handsome man I had ever seen. He looked like the British actor, Roger Moore, with his Italian suit and shoes. We had no clue about designer fashions forty years ago, but he was still a snappy dresser.

As the intensity of my romantic week with Nasir culminated, he asked to see me privately. Unsuspecting, I slipped away for a short five or ten minutes from my family's watchful eyes.

While standing in the family driveway, he said, "I really want to marry you. I've talked to my parents, and they'll send the proposal, but I want to hear your answer first."

His mother and father had already approved, and a formal proposal was pending. His proposal floored me. I was so unprepared. I had no idea that he was that serious about me. I searched for a way to get out of the situation gracefully.

Not wanting to offend, I offered to check with my parents. As their only daughter, I explained, I couldn't risk offending them if they didn't approve.

"I'm only sixteen," I said. "I'll check with my parents. If they say yes, we have a chance."

He was upset, jumped into his car, and peeled away. It was a foreboding of his anger, a red flag I didn't recognize.

Later, my father said, "I don't want to make any long-term commitments. You're going with us to Canada, and he's staying here with two years in medical school left. When he's done, if you two are still interested, then I'm okay with it."

Abu always knew how to handle a situation appropriately.

We had a long-distance romance that was quite cute. I would secretly take coins and go to the phone booth and call him. He would send me chocolates and I would send him American CDs. The courting period was very romantic, and as I recall it now, my heart glows and I smile.

We were married in West Pakistan in a traditional Pakistani ceremony. Five hundred guests attended the elegant and extravagant week-long festivities. I was only nineteen then.

Age 19 - September 1983 – Karachi – Fire Walk

Soon after my week-long wedding in Pakistan, my mother told me for the first time that I need to do the fire walk. When I was seven, a rose thorn went in my leg and I could not walk for three months. She prayed to God that if I walked again she would make me walk on fire.

I was so angry at her for making me do something I did not ask for. But having faith in God and respecting my mother's wishes, I went to do the fire walk on tenth of *Muharram* (a very important day in the Islamic calendar. It marks the day that the prophet's grandson, Imam Hussain, was martyred). I was 19 and looking out the window where the coals were ignited. I saw the sparks coming out from all that red burning coal.

The belief is that Imam Hussain's sacrifice for humanity was so strong that walking on fire is trivial. There were a lot of other people with me and we were all psyched to do the fire walk. We believed that if we walked in the name of God and humanity we would not burn our feet. Well sure enough, I walked and did not burn my feet. Whatever you believe the mind and body achieves. That was my first lesson in starting to believe in myself.

Our Commitment

Nasir was a very bright man and still is. He's a type A personality; once he makes up his mind, he then follows through.

There was chemistry between us. Life seems to sprinkle that liberally when there are lots of gifts and things to learn as a couple. It gets us to persist and work through the relationship challenges.

Our saving grace was the deep love we shared, and the commitment to make our marriage work. Because it was my choice, I decided to make it work. I believed a committed marriage is the key to a successful marriage.

AGE 21 – Vancouver, Canada – 1985 Not Speaking Up

It used to be that when my husband, Nasir, and I were driving, for example to a party, and we got lost, he would never ask for directions. I would say, "You need to stop and ask." He would get upset and say, "Either you do this one hundred percent, or let me". I would go into my old shutdown of not speaking up. The next time that we were in the same situation and lost, I would not speak up even if I knew where to go. What's the point anyway, I thought? It was better to shut down, than to speak up and cause a rift.

I even did this when I had a miscarriage. I was living in Vancouver at age twenty-one. Nasir was in Ohio doing his studying and living with his brother, Zakir. I told Nasir on the phone that I was bleeding, and he told me to go to the hospital. I told my mom, and took myself to the hospital for the D & C. After, I drove myself home. I told them when I got back, but no one said anything. Not, "I'm so sorry." Nothing. I wondered, 'will I ever have a child?'

I came home and seemed so super capable. My 'I need-to-prove' myself tape was running. My husband didn't say anything, my sisters-in-law didn't say anything. My mom didn't say anything. It was not that they didn't love me, they just didn't know how to communicate about intimate issues.

No Matter How Big or Small – Resolve Your Past

This message is for all women that have had miscarriages, and abuse, and are incomplete with their past. I am now completing it while I write this book over thirty years later. It is important to resolve the past, no matter how big or small it is. It is affecting you in the background and you don't even know about it. It is a block in your energy flow when it is unresolved.

It all ties together. The first time that I had my period, mom did not say anything. The first time that I had a miscarriage, no one said anything. The first time that I shared my abuse with my mom, nothing was said. I made a decision to figure out life all by myself.

It has created a super capable and powerful me, and now I realize that it is not necessary to do it all alone. I started questioning and looking for answers – just like you right now.

How Our Expectations Changed

After the first two years of marriage, the honeymoon was over. Our expectations of each other changed.

It was a lot for him to adjust to a new culture and medical system. He disconnected to cope with it all. He was always pre-call, post-call, or waiting to be called. Throughout his residency, he was sleeping if he wasn't working. I was so paranoid of sleeping by myself that I used to make my own call schedule where I was going to sleep when my husband was on call.

For two days, I'd wait for him to come home. When he was back, he went straight to sleep until he went back to work again. This pattern drove me crazy and made me angry. His perspective was, "I don't even get to sleep."

I'd think, "I waited for two days for you to come home, and now I have to sit at home and watch you sleep?" There was no time for love. I didn't have a social life or someone to confide in and have fun with.

I felt abandoned and betrayed. My 'happily ever after' seemed to have sunk like a wedding cake without the baking soda. I was miserable and made little effort to hide it. The little time we had was spent bickering. I was filled with angry tears and judgment while he was depleted, exhausted, and unable to meet my needs.

I'm sure he was as frustrated by my irrational behavior as I was with his. We were shut down and triggered by one another. Neither of us understood why.

Our problems grew. He felt that I did everything half-assed. At nineteen, I had enjoyed freedom, not discipline and structure as he had growing up.

His expectation of how a woman should be was formed from this only female role model in his life, his mother. She had five sons to raise; she was organized like the military. She was disciplined, with no femininity. Even fifty years ago, she wore pants and a shirt instead of traditional dresses. She developed masculine energy to contain the vibrant exuberance and mischievous energy of the six men in her home. She was an amazing woman.

I was unhappy, crushed, and constantly judging of everyone around me. I judged Nasir for not being there. How could he do this to me? Since I was insecure inside, I could not even trust him fully, and doubted his every action.

Age 29, West Virginia – summer of 1993
Our Family Grew

In order to secure our green cards, we moved to West Virginia in the summer of 1993. During this time, our in-laws were living with us and I gave birth to my third child. Needless to say, it was a stressful time for me having to cope with three kids and in-laws.

Nasir's residency ended, yet the hours were still demanding. The three children we created with a blessed ongoing passion filled my days and years with joy and a commitment to wonderful mothering.

The children and I developed a closeness that I'd always dreamed of, accepting and sharing joy and suffering alike. I was there for them totally. I made every effort to keep my communication open and accessible as my kids grew up. Yet, in my mind, I was still empty much of the time.

I was angry and convinced that it was Nasir's fault that I suffered. If only he was home more, then I'd be happy. I ruminated over the lack of a relationship between him and the children. It frustrated me, and I was stymied in my efforts to fix it.

What bothered me the most was that even when he made the effort to join us, he was physically present but not emotionally? He was preoccupied in his mental world, but not involved in ours.

I worked on our social scheduling and festivities as hard as I had on my studies. I excelled in perfect parties. I was a consummate hostess and coordinator. I found joy in serving and being in the limelight. But, I was a social queen with low self-esteem.

My constant judging and fear made it impossible for me to see that responsibility for my happiness lay inside of me. My absentee mother and husband made me overcompensate as a mother, a daughter, and a wife. Still, these were all important experiences in my path to freedom.

In general, we duplicate the patterns that were role modeled to us when we were growing up. I took a vow to break that pattern in my family. But, I was conflicted. My inner vision and my outer reality weren't matching up. That inner conflict took up a lot of energy. Conflict occupied space in my mind and body; it was blocking meaningful prosperity and enjoyable relationships. It was getting in the way of my living a healthy, happy, prosperous, and peaceful life.

I Began to Reinvent Myself

When we are reinventing, we start looking at different areas of our lives. We look at our key relationships, thoughts, and beliefs that are affecting us today. We explore how we judge ourselves and sabotage our goals, realizing what stories we make up from our past.

Figuring out where my issues began and who I'd been all my life became my life's passion. What were my daily thought processes? What did I say to myself on a daily basis? These answers were the brush with which I was painting my reality. I've learned that taking one hundred percent responsibility for all of this frees me to experience self-mastery.

I lived a good life even before I began the self-work that has liberated me. I had a big house, a big car, and all of the luxuries you can think of. You might wonder, "What was her problem?"

The problem was that my inner dialogue about myself was fear based from past experiences. It affected my relationships deeply. I believed that if my relationships didn't work, then nothing in my life would. I was determined to pursue happiness in my life, so I started taking responsibility for my own thoughts and actions. Then things started to shift. The intention to change was the first step.

Age 33 Vancouver, Canada – June 1996

My brother's death

My forty-year-old brother passed away unexpectedly from a heart attack while playing cricket. We were getting together for a family reunion in Vancouver, but the celebration became a mourning. His death triggered my childhood fear of sudden death from when I had lost my cousins. I became frozen with a fear that yet another loved one would die, or even myself. I went through the motions and cared for my family and their needs, but inside I was numb and tense. I was waiting for the other shoe to drop without really understanding why.

Unfortunately, our lives are self-fulfilling prophecies based on mistaken beliefs. We're the ones who are creating our circumstances, and then we make choices that prove ourselves right.

My parents were in Pakistan at the time, and my brothers and I were in Vancouver. Suddenly, I had to grow up and become the backbone and strength for them. I had to make arrangements and support my dad in his grief.

My brother's four daughters were young, and I took a vow to be there for them, to be close and give them the guidance. I felt my brother would have given if he were alive. They have grown up to be remarkable women. I'm honored to be their aunt.

My parents stepped up and took on the responsibility of caring for Saleem's family. It was a wake-up call for us all. Perhaps my three brothers: Tasleem, Shameem, and Nasim, are still awakening to their own health issues, at their own perfect pace. Saleem's sudden heart attack and diabetes helped me realize that I have to take care of myself more sweetly and diligently now.

We're still recovering from our loss and grief, and I'm working hard to release the extra weight of sadness. Together, we're healing as a family, waking up in the manner and pace that we're able to manage at the time.

Sometimes, we want our family members to transform and quickly listen to their inner voice. They're slow to change, we believe. We're tormented when they don't listen to our well-intentioned suggestions. We suffer as much as they do when we judge them. I wondered what I could do.

I'm still on my own transformational path, and I need to give others the freedom to choose to learn their life lessons on their own paths. Our addictions and coping mechanisms differ. Some of us over-achieve while others eat away the pain that we feel. We smoke, drink, or wrestle with any multitude of addictions. Regardless of the manifestation, the kindness of loving ourselves and each other is the only medicine that frees us forever.

ACTION STEP: Releasing Fear by Taking Accountability

1. Get your notebook and a cup of tea.
2. Write a list of people with whom you would like to improve your relationship.
3. What's missing from each of those relationships?
4. Where is it possible for you to take responsibility for your part with each one of them?
5. What fears that you identified in the first chapter are affecting these relationships?
6. How can you personally be accountable and change so that the relationship will change?

As you let go of layers of fear, you will free up the space for love and freedom.

ACTION STEP: Breathing Exercise to Release Fear

This is a simple technique for letting go of your fears and breathe deeply and slowly. In your mind, imagine each fear is being held in your chest. On each outbreath, breathe out one fear, imagine it leaving your body, perhaps your outbreath is a color. Notice how much calmer and freer you feel. Move on to the next fear. Keep going until you have released as many fears as is right for you at this time.

Chapter 3 How Judgment Hurts Us

"If you feel incomplete, you alone must fill yourself with love in your empty, shattered space."

- Oprah Winfrey

Fear of Judging

One day, I was listening to Dr. Wayne Dyer's CD on judgment while driving my car, and it reminded me of my own story when I was traveling to Karachi, Pakistan. I was in an airport in Karachi, having just landed from the United States. I went to the bathroom where there are poor female attendants who clean and hand you toilet paper and towels to dry your hands. You're supposed to tip them.

I thought, "Why am I going to tip her? Why can't she get a job? She looks healthy and fit." I decided not to tip her.

While I walked out and waited for my luggage to arrive, I started feeling icky inside. I realized that I was judging her for what she was doing. She worked in a stinky bathroom all day, hoping for a tip so that she could take that money home to her children and feed them. What did I know about her life anyway? Maybe she had a husband who died, or maybe she had a life filled with abuse.

I returned and tipped her a hundred rupees. That was a lot of money for her and no hardship for me. She was very happy. The smile on her face made me think twice about judging people on the street.

Slowly, I learned. Who am I to judge people who are doing what they can to survive? They're God's children. How can I love them for who they are?

There's not a single bad person, just bad behavior. It took me a long time to realize that God doesn't create anyone bad. We all arrive pure and innocent. We just acquire bad behaviors. We can stay as clean and pure as we were born, remembering the essence of our loving selves.

God loves us all equally. We come from divine love and we remain essentially good. It's not our essence that's affected when we sin or miss the mark. We make mistakes, yet we're essentially always good and lovable. I learned to focus on this truth and began to see the inherent value of each soul and situation by focusing less on the illusions of what I thought was valuable.

Started to Look for Love in Everyone and Everything

Even a suicide bomber who takes his life and the lives of people around him is inherently good. I found that instead of judging, giving love and spreading love helps heal the reasons that drove them to do what they did. When someone can't feel love, they don't value their lives or others. Whatever thoughts arrive, no matter what the question is, I've found that the real answer is love.

If we can come from a place of love and learn to love everything, we can create anything. Shifting my point of view so that I was no longer bringing anything forward from my past was a big struggle. With deep commitment, I did it. Whatever happened was in the past. It doesn't have to be my future. Becoming complete with my past is where I've found forgiveness. It's a big deal.

Until I forgave from my heart, I couldn't free myself and be complete, free to create differently. I have learned to look back with compassion. Now, when I review the past, I don't have any attachments. When I think of my abusers, I don't have anger. I forgive them and send them love. They did the best that they could, given their situation. If they knew differently, they would have done differently. They weren't bad people; they just had bad behaviors.

For most of my life, I was afraid of what people would think of me if they knew about my abuse. What if no one loved me if they knew? I put on a mask that projected only what I wanted people to see. I was judging myself in anticipation of others judging me.

I knew that I was becoming free of the past when I noticed that my thoughts about myself were changing. Instead of judging myself on a daily basis, I became more loving and accepting of who I was. The funny thing was, the less I judged others, the less I felt judged!

Judgment is the Core of Codependency

Judging comes from our own deep insecurities about our self-worth. I feel that we're constantly judging: what people wear or don't wear, what they're saying, or what accent they use. I often judged people because of what they wore. Their presentation and style was a clear rank of success for me. We judge a woman who wears a hijab. I never wore one, but I have a huge respect for the women who do.

I used to judge people who were overweight because I thought it meant they were irresponsible, didn't take care of their health, and that they didn't look good. To me, looking good was an essential element of life.

As long as we are judging, we cannot be loving. Judging comes from fear, and loving comes from freedom. I feel it is difficult for fear and freedom to coexist.

Judgment can catch us like a trap door and we can fall down the rabbit hole of the ego's delight. We're caught in Never Never Land. Or is it Wonderland? It's not so wonderful to be in. This results in codependency, an addiction to a person, place, or situation outside of us that we try to control or manage because our life has become unmanageable.

Judgment is the foundation of Stephen Karpman's drama triangle, which explains codependency well. Karpman studied under Eric Berne, the father of transactional analysis.

As Karpman explains, we have a tendency to take on destructive roles when dealing with conflict. We become the victim, the rescuer, or the persecutor. When we look at another and decide they're wrong, we automatically shift ourselves into that same level of consciousness. This sets up karma, or cause and effect, which guarantees that we're going to be playing the other side of that same drama soon, this lifetime or another.

Why is this important? It has to do with noticing when you're reaching for the mask that hides the judgment in your life. You feel justified when you play these roles unconsciously. Becoming conscious gives you clues when the unconscious voices confuse your clarity.

You tell yourself, "I did it for their own good. They need me to survive. What would they do without me?" Indeed. Perhaps they would learn to thrive. These are the voices of the Rescuer. If this feels familiar, you might look into codependency literature, such as *Codependent No More* by Melody Beattie.

"It's not my fault. If only they wouldn't have. They're always doing (or not doing) this to me." These are the cadences of the victim melody.

Persecutors say, "I'll teach them. I'll get them back. I'll make him see that I'm right and he's not."

Interestingly, we can play all three parts in overlapping roles in our lives, dancing between triangulating relationships. Karpman's Drama Triangle can help you begin to see the ego's subtle justifications for its actions. Controlling and manipulating are favorite foods for feeding the hungry ego mentality. If this resonates with you, I encourage you to dig deeper into his work.

Once I Stopped Judging and Started Loving

I now have three grown children: a beautiful daughter, and two handsome sons. For me, the most important thing about being a parent was choosing to be present for my kids while they were growing up. By contrast, my husband Nasir would leave at six a.m. and come home at ten p.m. Athletic games and recitals were not part of his life. He felt that his role was to be our provider, which he did very well, and we flourished financially.

I was upset that he wasn't there for us. To resolve that tension and the differences in our values, I started asking questions. I became a seminar junkie, going to one after the other, trying to figure out life. In the process, the seminars I attended offered CEU hours (credits for university). I decided to submit them all, along with my life experience, to an online University, where I was thrilled to discover that I had met most of the graduation requirements for a doctorate.

After a final year of online courses, I graduated with a doctorate degree in clinical hypnotherapy. The degree gave me credentials to serve others, which I already felt called to do. However, my intention was to prove myself and the motivating desire for being seen as a capable and complete human being was driven by my belief of not good enough. It was totally ego driven.

Imagine my surprise when I hung a framed PhD on my wall, but still didn't feel the love or respect that I was hoping it would bring. Finally, after searching for the truth high and low, behind every imaginable door, I discovered it was hidden securely within, as my own "true heart". Discovering self-love is an inside remodeling job, not just a piece of paper. I had been searching so frantically that I'd overlooked what was always inside.

I started resolving my past in my own mind through education and action.

I later learned that the university claimed to be accredited and it was not, so I stopped using title of PhD.

Tempering the Ego

I've learned to recognize my ego's judging voice when it shows up. Listening to ego can cause a fall from grace, which slams the golden gates of Eden shut. Being right costs peace of mind. As long as I'm one up or one down, I'm in a dualistic state that's based on ego. In heaven, all are accepted.

I have learned many ways of tempering my ego. I'm married to a physician, and both of our egos need to be right. Early in our marriage, we were in constant arguments, trying to prove one another wrong. A wounded ego is dangerous. It wants to counter attack like an angry wounded animal. I feel we all have wounded egos and are trying to make up for something in the past. And it has nothing to do with the other person.

As one of the books on the relationships that I read that really helped me was *The 5 Love Languages* by Gary Chapman. I learned that we are all speaking different languages, and mine is "receiving gifts", and "spending time". My husband's love language was "act of service". We both expressed our love in completely different languages that were foreign to one another, and we both felt like we were not being loved properly.

In learning to communicate better, I figured out that it's better to ask questions than tell people what to do. Because that does not empower them. Asking questions lets them explore the possibility within. Ask open-ended questions. For example:

What can I do to improve our relationship?

How do you want me to express love?

How can I be supportive?

Learning to heal and let go of the ego is a whole life journey. The ego is an illusion. It has no power. All of its positions and efforts to manage outside people, places and things are just an indication of how out of control we feel within.

We cannot do our spiritual work and make progress while we have an unmanageable ego. Recognizing our ego's subtle acts, and learning to lift the illusion of its control and power struggle while gracefully repositioning, is the art of conscious living.

The job of the ego is to protect and make you look good. Shutting down or retaliation are two of its favorite tricks. I've learned that recognizing when I'm shut down or trying to make myself look good is the first step. Then, I slow down and reflect on my intention. Is the gift I'm seeking to give motivated by love, or my ego?

These are the steps that have allowed me to shift the very focus and structure of my life. Learning to listen within has been another huge gift.

Age 40 - Detroit, Michigan – May 2003

Intention Is Powerful

I was driving from Detroit to Chicago to attend yet another seminar in a search for the peace and freedom that I desperately wanted but didn't yet feel.

I was turning forty that year and I believed that it was a pivotal year for me. I was determined to begin awakening my mighty spirit within. I made an intention that year to change my life.

On my way to Chicago, I picked up a CD from Barnes & Noble for my four-hour drive. As I entered the store, it seemed to leap off the table and into my hands: Richard Carlson's *You Can Be Happier, No Matter What*. This, I thought, was the answer to my prayers.

I listened intently to two CDs on the way to Chicago, and two coming back. It dawned on me that the answers to my questions and my happiness switch were located inside of me.

Before that, I thought that the answers were found outside. "My husband Nasir doesn't love me. He doesn't have time for me. If only people understood me. If only Nasir wouldn't behave that way. If only my mother was more expressive and had been there for me, life would be good. If only I had more of whatever my ego thought I needed, I would be happy."

On and on the voice within would complain. I was judging everyone in my life. I was blaming the whole world for my unhappiness and it wasn't working. Everything was exhaustingly externalized.

That day, driving seventy miles an hour on I-94 on my way back from Chicago, I was sobbing most of the way. I must have been watched over to have been able to drive straight. While my heart was breaking open like a nut I'd shelled away, my ears strained for the next words and the solution I desperately needed emerged.

"The bottom line," Carlson said in his last CD", is that happiness is a choice."

"What?!" I thought, "Did I hear that right?"

I forgot to sob, as I was so startled.

"You can have the most awful life, and you can choose to be happy. You can even have an abusive life, and you can choose to be happy."

"Oh my God," I said slapping my head. "It's a choice. I can't blame my husband anymore. I can't blame and judge my circumstances anymore." I was stunned.

I believe that in that instant, my world turned upside down and inside out. I realized I had a choice, and that choice could be happiness. Happiness isn't based on my environment or circumstances. A light bulb went on in my head, turning me on in a quest for happiness. The switch had been right inside of me all along, just waiting to be switched on. I thought answers to happiness were found outside. Now, I realized our inner world determines what we see.

Every action has an equal and opposite reaction, so are you going to be the action or the reaction today? Intentions are very powerful, so what intentions are you ready to make today?

ACTION STEP: Defeating Judgment by Letting Go of Expectations

Find a private place, and perhaps light a candle for inspiration and clarity. Look at the list of people that you created in the action step, **Releasing Fear by Taking Accountability,** at the end of chapter two.

For each person on the list, honestly answer the following questions in your journal.

1. How have you been judging in your relationships?

2. Can you choose to be happy regardless of your circumstances?

3.what can you give up today?

4. Is being right more important to you than being happy

5. Who should you call today, to start making up for lost time in your life?

Now take deep breaths, and as you breathe out, release your judgments, and your fears one at a time. Practice this a few times. Coming back to your breath every time is the key.

Chapter 4 How and Why Do We Self-Sabotage?

"Our beliefs can move us forward in life, or they can hold us back."

- Oprah Winfrey

Same Old Same Old

Why do we continue to find ourselves in the same situations with different people playing the same roles? Self-sabotage keeps us stuck because it's familiar. Despite affirmations, best intentions, visualizing, and therapy, we sometimes find ourselves stuck in ways we don't understand.

The ego wants to blame and shift responsibility. It wants to project our issue outside of us when the power to shift happens internally. Liberation occurs when we shift the focus from outside to inside, refocusing our mind to find the freedom we seek.

I have experienced self-sabotage in different areas of my life. I also see it often in my hypnotherapy practice, where many client's main concerns are to stop smoking, and to lose weight. I used to self-sabotage my health and fitness goals all the time.

My personal goals included working out five times a week, and eating more veggies and fruits, lean meats, and palm-sized portions.

Then, I'd commit to events, which often included food from Friday evening through Sunday, in addition to socializing with my husband.

Sometimes, we're out until 1:15 a.m. When I'm too tired in the morning to rise and exercise. I grab a sweet roll and then suddenly I'm headed down a dead-end path for my weekend eating.

When we dine out and Nasir orders, the French fries arrive and once they're in front of me, they're too tempting.

Instead of saying, "He can eat what he wants and I'll chose healthy," I think, "Why should I deprive myself? If he can eat fries, I'll eat fries too." Then, he orders my favorite dessert (perhaps my sweetness reminds him). It's easy for me to blame my husband for ordering French fries and apple pie with vanilla ice cream.

Biology of Belief author Bruce Lipton says that your environment plays a big part in keeping your commitments. When your environment presents donuts and French fries, your brain emits a powerful chemical that draws you away from the long-term commitment and payoff of fitness, and moves toward the voice that says, "I want to eat it. I must have it. Give it to me now!"

When we look at trigger foods, our pleasure center is activated, and the addictive lure of sugar and carbs knock us off our wagon. Sugar is the number one addiction in the United States. Robbed of all nutritious qualities, refined sugar or, worse yet, high-fructose corn syrup, manipulates our insulin levels, and creates a roller-coaster energy and emotional ride.

We are creatures of habit and we can change our lives by changing our beliefs. What are beliefs? All recurring thoughts and stories become our beliefs. For me it was my belief that I was not good enough and spent half my life proving myself right.

According to Lipton, "Positive thoughts have a profound effect on our behavior and genes, but only when they are in harmony with subconscious programming. Negative thoughts have an equally powerful effect. When we recognize how these positive and negative beliefs control our biology, we can use this knowledge to create lives filled with health, happiness, peace, and freedom." (Lipton, *Biology of Belief*.)

I've learned to stop being judgmental, focus on my own self-control, and be okay with what is while coming from a place of love. I've learned that whatever you resist persists. When I judge him, I get more insensitive behavior.

I also love myself more. It's only when we accept where we are that we can transform. When I love myself, it's easier for others to feel more accepting of me. One of my teachers told me to accept people where they are, not where you want them to be. This suggestion really helped me when I felt triggered by other people to accept them where they are and not expect them to think and behave like me. I am not responsible for fixing anyone. Everyone is doing their best with the resources they have. We are all on our own journey from fear to freedom.

Females with a History of Abuse Tend Toward Self-Sabotage

Women can use their weight to protect themselves. Just like an armor to shield their vulnerability from abuse.

Women sometimes emotionally overeat. Whenever I was triggered by my husband, I would go into the fridge and say, "Oh, what can I eat to soothe my pain?" We all have different triggers in our lives, what are yours?

In my current state of mind, this happens to me very rarely. It's not completely gone, life still keeps happening. But now, I'm aware of myself and before I overindulge, I talk to myself and ask, "What's going on?"

"Oh, I'm so angry!"

"Who are you angry with?

"Oh, myself."

I self-assess and come out of the story.

Being present to my needs keeps me from acting out impulsively. When we repeat the same painful story over and over again in our mind we tend to overindulge and lose control.

My Client's Self-Sabotage Story

I once had a client who came in for pain management. Her pain was eased during our session, and we anchored new ways of managing it. When she returned, the pain was back, and she was complaining.

I asked her, "What's going on that you keep going back to this pain?"

"Well, if I'm in pain, my husband pays attention to me," she answered. "He cooks for me, drives me places, and nurtures me. When I feel better, he stops paying attention to me."

It's easy to see her logic.

The secondary gain was her husband's attention. The primary gain was feeling no more pain. It was overcome by the secondary gain of her husband's care taking. At some level, she got more reward from the attention. She would rather be in pain with his attention than be lonely with no pain.

Once she had the awareness, she could choose. "Am I going to stay in pain because he pays attention to me? Or can I request that we connect in other ways that meet both of our needs more comfortably? Either way, we're taking responsibility for our choice."

I suggested to my client that she could be pain free, healthy, and vibrant and still be able to attract her husband's attention. I suggested this while she was in the theta state (The theta state describes brain waves between 4 and 7.5 cpm. This is the optimum state for meditation and hypnosis and is present in REM or dream sleep. It is a good place from which to learn and change). This prompted her to have a conversation in person with her husband.

She shared with him that she loves that he takes her to her doctor appointments and asked that he continue to do loving things with her. Now, she's in a different space. She's shifted the role of victim by becoming creatively empowered. She and her husband get along much better, enjoying quality time.

What Do I Do When I Blow It?

Children who have been abused tend to self-sabotage, so that they can prove to themselves that they were never good enough to make it.

When we're self-sabotaging, our ego is living either in the future or the past, not in the moment. This is one of the clues that points to the possibility that our ego is driving our bus temporarily; lamenting about what has happened or worrying about what's yet to be.

When I step back into gratitude, I'm embraced by the Divine Mother within me. She's compassionate, kind, and consistent. She isn't mean, berating, or shaming. She loves me, and loves others through me, even when we might be temporarily fearful or out of sorts. Being kind with myself has grown compassion in me so that I can be kind in the world.

When you're in fear, you get stressed. Your mind races and your heart beats faster. Adrenaline kicks in, and after repeat cycles of high blood sugar surges, followed by low blood sugar crashes, the adrenals can burn out.

When my thoughts creates the feeling of intense fear, and then my mind reacts to that fear and creates more of it. It's a vicious cycle.

Dropping Control: Letting GO

One of my past pressures was keeping my keen sense of fear at bay by controlling how everything was going. I had such anxiety that I couldn't let things unfold, but had to micromanage their direction. Letting go was hard for me.

What would happen if I stopped doing things? What if no one picked up the slack? What would *they* think if things didn't come off perfectly? Besides that, who was going to admire me when it all came off faultlessly? I had to constantly prove to my not good enough self that I can do it.

One of the greatest gifts I ever gave myself or family was the ability to relax and be at peace with whatever was happening. Relaxing my standards gave us all the room to enjoy one another and notice that we were very fortunate and safe. Even when things didn't go the way that we planned. I began to believe in serendipity - the gift of grace from the Universe.

I began to flourish in the chaos of my family affairs, in my immediate home and during the large Muslim vacation retreats of my extended family. Sometimes, three dozen of us would gather in a home filled with impromptu comings and goings amidst three formal meals a day. Workers would take care of the details, and we were blessed to simply be and enjoy each other's company. Our most demanding activities were shopping and deciding what to wear for dinner that evening.

Only when I relaxed my self-imposed standards and need to control did I became centered, peaceful, and trusting. I believed that whatever the Universe was creating was completely safe and exactly what I needed.

Beginning to notice rather than react became a tranquil stepping back. As my children grew and moved from our family home into their own busy lives, rather than lose my identity, I began to flourish. I was nourished by the influx of what arrived.

No one had ever told me directly that letting go could open up so much more. Perhaps it was Abu's remarkable ability to walk away from all he had built so that we could move and be free. Perhaps that has helped me feel safe to lean into and learn how to release.

Getting Out of the Darkness

Over the last thirteen years, I progressed and then slid back into the blame pattern, falling into the same hole again and again. Sometimes, I'd stay stuck miserably in that hole for three days or more, blaming everyone and everything. Then I would realize that I didn't want to be there anymore. I'd make efforts to get a mentor, a coach, or a friend to give me a hand so that I could climb up and out. The amazing thing was that the way out of the hole was always a shifting inside, not outside of me!

Over the years, I managed to reduce the time I spent in the hole. It became two days, then one. It shifted recently to a couple of hours, and then only a few minutes. I'd recognize that I didn't even want to get into the hole anymore. I learned to walk around it. I don't fall for it any more.

The irony is that I always thought that I was shoved into that dark place. It took a long time of repeated self-awareness to realize that my own fears were tripping me up.

We all have a dark side. Everything is light and dark, yin and yang. That's where the awareness part comes in. You must become aware of your life patterns and your habitual daily habits that don't get you where you want to go. If your dark side is still buried in your subconscious, then you cannot access it or change it.

When you become conscious of your subconscious, then you can change. Awareness is the first step, being aware of where you are and why you're there. What choices got you there?

The Tyranny of More – What Are You Attached To?

I was feeling at peace. In fact, I was really in bliss. Out of the blue, the picture of a home came in the mail. I thought, "Hey, maybe the Universe wants me to see this home. It looks really good on paper." So, I called my realtor and we went to see it. It was on a lake and I've always wanted to live on a lake. To me, water represents peace, tranquility, and a sense of belonging.

It was beautifully constructed, six bedroom suites with a bathroom and sitting room in every bedroom. I fell in love at first sight. I started visualizing how I'd be entertaining guests there. I scheduled another appointment and took my entire family the next day.

They all loved it, and my daughter, being funny said, "It's only a mile above our budget, Mom."

"I'm going to buy it with cash from the book that I'm writing, which will be a number one bestseller. The Universe is listening to me now! I know I can create magic."

There's a paradox about wanting material things in the future and owning the complete ecstasy of Loving Oneness in the present moment.

The more my story ran me, the more I became aware of another layer of "should's" and my past creeping up on me. "I'm not good enough to afford this home. If only I was making a million dollars on my own, without my husband's support, I could afford this house. I wouldn't need anybody for approval for funding."

"Besides," my ego continued, "My husband really doesn't approve of me and my continual education. He's still waiting for me to make it."

I spoke for him in my mind, "All this education. When is it finally going to pay off?"

In fact, I made up all kinds of imagined conversations about things he'd never said. Finally, I heard him summarize, "If she only did what she learned, she'd be successful."

In the meantime, I was getting really anxious and uptight. I skipped my prayers and meditation because I was mad at myself and God. I was so mad one day, I decided I wasn't even going to pray. "Why am I not getting what I want, God? Why are you not giving me the abundance of money that I'm supposed to get? Why did you show me this house in the first place, if you didn't want me to have it?" I demanded.

My husband didn't know any of this. I wasn't sleeping at night by this time. We were already living in a beautiful, blessed home overlooking a serene setting. My family was happy and peaceful. Most of the time, we have no financial burden because Nasir is such an amazing provider.

If I moved into a two-million-dollar home, it would be completely stressful and insane. My desire for a super mansion on a lake overrode all logic and reason. It wiped out my attitude of gratitude.

Nasir didn't have a clue, but he did notice that I wasn't being myself. "What are you stressed out about?" he finally asked.

"I cannot get that house out of my head." He just smiled and said, "We cannot afford it", and walked away.

On the Third Day, I Had a Revelation

I finally asked myself, "Where is the end to this? When will you feel that you have enough?" I realized that I already have enough and that I am enough, right here and now.

I prayed.

I meditated.

I exercised.

It was a breakthrough. I wanted a home that was three times as expensive as the one in which I'm currently happily living in. Stuff doesn't make us happy, our thoughts make us happy! I'd learned this before, right? The ego is a persistent and greedy pest that plagues humanity. The more we grow in our collective consciousness, the subtler its falsehood can be.

Attachments are always about ego, and as Dr. Wayne Dyer, author of *The Power of Intention,* says, "Whenever we are in EGO, we are Edging God Out".

Islam teaches about detachment, and releasing desire. We can get so caught up in material possessions that satisfy our need to look good and be successful. The lake that I desired was really the peaceful tranquil emotions that I created from inside. I'm the lake.

No matter how far we climb on the ladder of our lives, we notice a chattering little monkey mind, called ego clinging to our back.

"Who do you think you are?" It pulls you down a rung. Then whispers in your left ear, "You're *nobody* since you don't have a two-million-dollar home." Then, in a moment of humanness, or amnesia, you forget that you are a beloved child of a Mother who owns the cosmos. How silly to forget and how human to forgive yourself. How divine to remember once again that we are all one.

I am honored to have readers as dear to my heart as you. We have listened and learned together through this book. It is all the validation that I need to be successful and free. It' was my deepest desire to share my story to empower other women reinvent themselves.

ACTION STEP: Reinvent

Adapted from the book "What You Think of Me is None of My Business," by Terry Cole Whittaker

Observe

Where is your life now?

What patterns have you adapted from your past?

Do you feel that fear is holding you back from living the life of your dreams?

Choose

Accept that you created this life pattern. Now you have a choice to choose differently. What new choices are you ready to take on today?

Give Up Blame

Where in your life are you judging yourself and others? Stop judging and start loving.

Create A New Life

Repeat these affirmations daily:

I am successful and free.

I am enough.

I am loveable.

ACTION STEP: Healing Through Drawing

One of the books I have published is called *Insights to Tree Drawing*, and I use it to teach my clients to heal through their drawings.

First, draw a picture of where you are, in your pain and fear.

Second, draw a picture of what you think you need to get over this issue (they might draw a person, a therapist, a dog, etc.

Third, draw a picture of how a perfect life would look to you. What are you thinking, feeling, and saying? How are your days filled, and what are you learning, your perfect image of what life would look like with freedom and ease.

The subconscious will reveal things to you that you don't know. When you are drawing you can't lie. Ultimately, this work of art represents you, so capture whatever imagery comes to you and try not to judge your own work. There are no wrong answers in art.

STEP TWO
REPROGRAM

Chapter 5 Why Is Dealing with Stress Important?

"Every day brings a chance for you to draw a breath, take off your shoes, and dance."

- Oprah Winfrey

Learning to manage stress is important before we do the re programing.

When you are chronically stressed, you revert to your old habits and behaviors. By that, I mean your subconscious mind reverts to old patterns and programming because that's most familiar. When you are stressed you make bad choices.

The bigger the difference between how your environment is, and how you want it to be, the greater the stress. For example: when I come home from work, I like to come home to a clean, tidy, kitchen. But because I had six men living in the house, every time I came home, the kitchen sink was filled with dishes, the counters covered with food, and it was total chaos. My stress levels were high from the moment I entered my own home, because my environment was not conducive to my goals. A messy house was a major trigger for me.

No matter what the issues my clients come to me with, I teach them stress management first so that they can cope with their current environment. As the gap between their desire and their environment decreases, the stress decreases.

What Is Stress?

Wikipedia defines stress as "a specific response by the body to a stimulus, like fear or pain, which disturbs or interferes with the normal physiological equilibrium of an organism.

It is important to be aware of stress in the human body. Long ago, when you saw a hungry beast in the wild, your body shot adrenaline through you. You prepared for "fight or flight." Your survival depended on killing or outrunning the beast.

The wild beasts have all become metaphors in modern times. Your boss may stress you out, and your body may give you a shot of adrenaline to fight or flee from that person – but you would lose your job if you did either of those things.

Most abused women have difficulties coping with stress. Managing your stress levels and sources of stress are critical and often overlooked. You cannot feel freedom if you are stressed out; those two entities cannot coexist.

Easy as ABC

I did my stress management certification from the National Guild of Hypnosis. Managing your stress is the key to release fear and find freedom.

I learned from Dr. Albert Ellis that it is our thoughts about our environment that cause stress in our lives. Dr. Ellis is a psychologist specializing in stress management and teaches the basics of interrupting undesirable outcomes.

Dr. Ellis taught me the **ABCs** of stress management. **A** is the adverse situation or event, **B** is our belief system, and **C** is the consequence.

Many times, we think that the adversity causes the consequences. We totally bypass our belief systems. We think that **A = C,** when, in fact, it's really **A + B = C.** Adding our belief systems to an adversity causes the consequences. Our beliefs are the filters that focus our outcomes. Beliefs are the root cause for reactions in our lives. Beliefs are formed by repeating the same thought over and over again.

Then, there's **D**, for dispute. When we dispute our beliefs about an adversity, it results in the consequence being different.

I used to be immersed in my story about my husband and how I was a victim of my circumstances. When I stopped this story, it freed me from running myself into the ground wondering, "What am I going to say next, and how will I say it? What if he says this next? Then what will I say?" I used to be doing the whole conversation for both of us in my head. Because I believed that I was the victim in our relationship.

How many times have you done that?

Now, when I have a conversation in my head, I interrupt my thoughts before they run away like a train without brakes. The stop sign stops the train from running away and causing a wreck.

Saying, "I'm ready to stop my thoughts", shifts your consciousness, allowing you to choose differently. The power of presence shifts outer events when you choose loving truth inside. It interrupts your thought patterns that you used to get stuck in so you can navigate around them and forge new paths.

For example, a client of mine came to me to stop smoking. She managed to it give up for a few years. But then the tragic death of her spouse was a new traumatic stress that caused her to go back to her old habit. She started smoking again. Managing stress is the key to keeping your actions aligned with your intentions.

Two people are standing underneath a roller coaster, and one is repeating in their head "Oh my goodness, this looks exciting and exhilarating and I can't wait to get on". The other is shaking and saying, "Oh my God, I'm going to die if I get on that roller coaster".

The roller coaster is the same, its their thought about the ride causing them anxiety or excitement. One person's happy experience may be the other's terror, based on their belief systems.

I have learned that there is no such thing as stress. This is because stress is a choice. You can choose to be stressed or not, based on your thought process. If you change your thoughts, you change your stress level. When a stressful thought occurs, you can yell "STOP!" and say to yourself "Thank you for sharing, and I choose to relax anyway." Dr. Dyer always said, "Everything starts with a thought. Change your thoughts, change your life."

100% Ability = 100% Response-ability

You are 100% responsible for your life! The brain is an amazing tool that can operate at one hundred percent efficiency when it's properly trained, harnessed, and following Divine mind's guidance. You accomplish this by taking one hundred percent responsibility for the thoughts you choose as you go through your days. To create a new habit and stop the old, negative mode of thinking, you need to replace it with new positive, productive thinking.

When you enter a spiritual spiral path, the Divine mind begins to think through you, and your surrender allows the Divine to choose for you. The Divine knows your real needs, and when you align with these solutions, your paths become pre-approved, easily and effortlessly.

You enter a zone of flow and peace, releasing the old story of how things needed to be. This gives you a new lease on life. It centers you in a Divine *now* which is empowering and perfect.

ACTION STEP: STOP Method

As a tool, learn to raise a bright red STOP sign in your mind and yell STOP internally. When things come to a complete halt, you can dispute them rather than act them out in the same habitually, self-destructive way.

When I ate to medicate, I would reach for the refrigerator door to avoid reaching inside to deal with my feelings. I learned to STOP and pause to feel what was happening, and began to lose weight as I lightened up emotionally. I repeated the affirmations below. Keep the following affirmations by your refrigerator and see if it works for you:

I am in control of what I eat

I am in control of when I eat

I am in control of how much I eat

Write the answers to these questions in your journal.

1. When thinking of an issue, are your thoughts really true?
2. Are your thoughts 100% accurate or exaggerated?

3. Did you make up stories about the event?

4. Separate the fact from your story and see them or the event with a different perspective as the mature you now,

NLP

Before we start, it might be useful to explain what Neuro Linguistic Programming (NLP) is. Richard Bandler, one of the co-founders of NLP, describes it as:

"A model of interpersonal communication chiefly concerned with the relationship between successful patterns of behavior and the subjective experiences (especially patterns of thought) underlying them" (Oxford English Dictionary).

The discipline is aimed at helping us all to understand how our brains respond to our thoughts and beliefs and to what happens to us (the neuro part). There have been breakthroughs in our understanding of how we organize our beliefs about the world (our map) and how we can change this map. By understanding how we use language and other forms of communication (the linguistic part) we can change our patterns of emotional behavior (the programming part).

When I used NLP to overcome my fears it was quick and easy.

ACTION STEP: Anchor of Relaxation

NLP guru, John Grinder, suggests that every night before going to sleep that you review your day and create a different possibility for responding to your worries and issues.

First, focus on your breathing. Then visualize a perfect outcome to your specific situation. See it in full color with sound and movement. Make it as realistic as possible, as if it has already happened. Then press your thumb and your index finger together as if you're squeezing a grape and anchor in this feeling of accomplishment with your favorite color and the word "relax".

Every night before going to bed, meditate on these higher outcomes as you fall asleep. Whatever your subconscious mind sees and believes, the body will achieve.

Chapter 6 How Can We Overcome Our Fears?

"Our beliefs can move us forward in life, or they can hold us back."

- Oprah Winfrey

This chapter has three sections, each of which is equally important for learning to overcome your fears.

1. Hypnosis
2. Inner Child Work
3. Past Life Regression

Hypnosis

Before I found hypnosis, I felt like a prisoner in a cage that I'd created. I was running in place like a hamster in a wheel. I was frustrated as I looked out of the bars and blamed everyone for my lack of freedom. I was stuck and hurting.

Hypnosis was exactly what I needed. It became the catalyst that started me on a journey of freeing myself from the confines of the hamster wheel. I had no idea how to begin, but because of that one thought, I had already begun.

To overcome my fears, I needed to align my conscious desires with my subconscious programming; to try something radically different than what hadn't been working all those years.

As I was going through my mail, I received a card about hypnosis classes in Lansing, Michigan. I said, "This is what God wants me to do. He is answering my prayers." To my surprise, when I told my husband that I wanted to become certified in hypnotherapy, he said he wanted to join me as well. That was the transition from fear to freedom in our relationship.

When you hear the word hypnosis, you may picture in your mind someone sitting in a chair, unable to move or speak freely, and no longer in control of their mind. That their control has been taken over by a hypnotist sitting nearby, giving them various, sometimes ridiculous or even harmful commands. Pretty scary! And yet, this description is how hypnosis is generally portrayed on television and in movies!

Three common misconceptions about hypnosis:

1) **Hypnosis is something done to you.** In reality, all hypnosis is self-hypnosis because you are always in control of your subconscious mind.

   The conscious mind is where logical and analytical thoughts and decision-making takes place. Subconscious mind is your auto-pilot. It tells you what to do based on your internal belief system that has been developed and reinforced over time by your memories and your responses to circumstances. You are not consciously aware of this belief system, but it has been assisting (or hindering) your survival and growth since birth.

Your subconscious mind will not let you do anything against your belief system, or without your consent. Thus, a hypnotherapist cannot convince your subconscious mind of anything without your conscious consent. Even with your consent, hypnosis is always about you making the effort to change your own subconscious mind. While an expert hypnotherapist can guide your subconscious mind and suggest how to change that belief system, they are only a facilitator, and you are the one who will do the work of changing your subconscious belief system.

2) **Hypnosis is like voodoo or something darkly supernatural.** On the contrary, hypnosis is such a natural process that you don't consciously notice it. The vast majority (90%) of what you do is based on your internal programming, your subconscious belief system that has developed over years of experience. There is nothing spooky or supernatural about making the conscious decision to:

—Gain a better understanding of your personal belief system (your subconscious programming)

—Determine whether your beliefs help or hinder your growth

—Change your belief system so that it truly works for you

3) **Hypnosis is for entertainment purposes only.** It is true that there are great stage performers displaying techniques of hypnosis before an audience. Unfortunately, public displays of hypnotism feed the misconception that hypnosis is about being controlled and that it's a performance that has only

entertainment value. This is simply untrue. Hypnosis is neither a game nor a spectacle, and it is completely accessible to everyone. Clinical hypnosis only helps change a person's behavior when the patient agrees to making that behavioral change.

What is Hypnosis?

Hypnosis is a naturally occurring state of deep relaxation, heightened focus, and heightened suggestibility. In this relaxed state, your conscious mind moves out of the way, and your subconscious mind is open to suggestion. You can change any belief system that holds you back from obtaining emotional healing or any other goals that you desire through hypnosis.

Hypnosis facilitates discovering the root causes of your behavior and eliminating limiting beliefs in your subconscious mind, which results in permanent changes in your behavior.

My work as a hypnotherapist involves three basic steps. I first help my patients to identify what subconscious beliefs keep them from moving forward. Is it fear? Anxiety? Doubt? Low self-esteem? I then help them to clarify in their conscious mind what new beliefs they want to replace their current beliefs. For example, they may want self-confidence, healing from past abuse, or to excel at public speaking.

First, I help my patients become calm and relaxed. It is in this state of calm relaxation where their conscious mind becomes quiet and their subconscious beliefs can be changed by my suggesting new beliefs in the form of guided imagery and visualization. The sub conscious mind sees in pictures only.

Using images is important because the subconscious mind bypasses language. New beliefs become firmly established in the subconscious mind through repetition over time (such as picturing an image of your goal each night before bed). In the course of a few weeks, new beliefs become stronger, and old ones fade away. Changes in your belief system result in permanent behavior changes.

Through hypnosis, you can change your perception of an incident that happened long ago. For example, my perception from my childhood abuse was that I must have been a bad girl. Through hypnosis, I was able to look at these events from a different perspective and was able to heal my own mind, body, and life.

Finally, hypnosis aligns your subconscious mind with what it is you consciously want to achieve. You can make a conscious goal to lose weight or overcome abuse, but if your subconscious mind is not in agreement, if you still believe that you should frequently reward yourself with sweets, your willpower alone will not overcome your core beliefs or result in permanent change.

How Do You Know You've Been Hypnotized?

When you are hypnotized, you will most likely experience the following:

- Your breathing slows down.
- Your eyes flicker.

- Your arms and hands feel a bit numb.

- You feel like you're in a snooze state — you hear everything, but you're so relaxed you don't want to bother to get up, even though you can get up if you desire, you can speak, and you are totally in control.

It's worth emphasizing that you can always choose to get up and walk away during a hypnosis session. I personally have never had a patient get up and leave during a session. In fact, numerous patients have told me that they felt like they've been in a massage session: very relaxed, safe, and in a healing mode.

Why Use Hypnosis?

The truth is that many medications only address disease or illness symptoms, leaving the root cause and problem unchanged. While the problem may be relieved temporarily, it cannot disappear permanently as long as the underlying belief system is unchanged. Most of my patients are referred to me by physicians. These patients have emotional issues that they have not healed, or addressed over many years.

Hypnosis addresses the root cause of limiting conditions such as fear, pain, anxiety, and stress — conditions which manifest as many types of illnesses. It provides an opportunity for changes in the subconscious mind that result in healing and permanent behavior change — allowing you to reach your goals!

In addition to addressing root causes, hypnosis enables you to heal your own subconscious mind *without having to confront the person who caused your harm.* Hypnosis changes your perception of any harm done to you (for example, you no longer see yourself as being at fault, a bad person, or a victim). You experience emotional release and healing so that you can achieve what you desire.

After a series of sessions with Kim, my hypnotherapist friend and fellow student, I began to feel lighter and lighter. Each time I left her office, I had the sensation of leaving behind emotional baggage that I no longer needed to carry around in my life.

Age 40 – Hypnotic Regression – 2003

Kim and I were practicing in class once, and she asked me what I wanted to work on.

"I notice that I'm afraid, really afraid, yet there's nothing that appears to be wrong. I can't figure out what's wrong with me." It felt awkward to share, and I was sure she was judging me. Yet I was determined to find out why I was feeling anxious all the time.

"Let's try the steps and see what we find." She seemed gentle and kind as she began to read the script we'd been given for a hypnotic regression.

"Take a deep breath and relax, and let me set the safe space for us to explore your experience. Let's go to the root cause of this intense fear," she read,

A few minutes later, I was descending, step by step, down an imaginary stairway; my mind slowed, my breath deepening as we went from ten to one. I moved into the hallway of my memory, and felt an invisible presence direct me to a door that had been securely closed for four decades.

I found myself at age five in my childhood house in Dacca, feeling numb, frozen from my solar plexus to my belly. It was like a rock had taken up permanent residence in my gut, and was pushing out my rib cage.

Yet there was nothing amiss. There were no warning signs from outside. The sky was clear. The room was quiet. Obviously, I was stuck and I didn't know why. Finally, as Kim went through the steps, a memory flashed in my mind:

I entered a dark room and a teenage boy was on top of me, his face was dark. A glimpse of my five-year-old self flashed in my mind. She was trapped, stuck, terrified. It was awful.

Kim assured my five-year-old mind that it was not my fault. There was nothing I could have done. She said, "Now push him away, and tell your five-year-old self that you will keep her safe and secure from now on". Hug her and kiss her and tell her you're going to love her just the way she is.

Coming back as my adult self, I did the balloon exercise (see below) to replace all that negative emotion with positive feelings of high self-esteem and self-confidence as I came up. As I emerged from the session, I felt a sense of peace, and deep relaxation. I felt good about myself for the first time in my life.

The Balloon Exercise

Imagine you are blowing up a balloon. Every time you blow the balloon you are blowing a negative emotion out of your mind and body, and into the balloon. Make the balloon bigger and blacker every time you release a negative emotion like fear, anger, hurt, guilt, or shame into the balloon. Imagine the negativity leaving your mind and body and entering the balloon.

Take the balloon out of your mouth and tie a knot. Release it into the sky and watch it go up, taking all the negativity from your mind and body with it, and getting smaller and smaller as it goes up into the sunlight. See the sunlight heal the negative energy, and the balloon disappear into the distance. Now, replace the void in your mind and body with love, peace, joy, and harmony.

It's Never Too Late to Have a Happy Childhood

We all have a child inside of us that needs to be championed. It's never too late to have a happy childhood. When we change our thoughts about our past events and abuse from self-blaming to self-healing, the shift happens. As we focus on new thoughts the old belief of not being good enough changes.

A belief creates a thought, a thought causes you to act, and your action determines your results.

As you change your thoughts, you start to take different actions – thus getting new results in your life. The bottom line is that, with hypnosis, you can change your feelings and beliefs about the abuse you experienced. This will then change your thoughts and actions. Then you will find freedom.

As I started feeling better about myself and stopped blaming the world for my problems, I started taking actions that moved me toward my goals instead of sabotaging my goals as I used to. My relationship with my husband changed to love and respect.

Connecting with Your Inner Child

Relax and find a comfortable space to sit. Close your eyes and imagine yourself as a child. Perhaps it was when you were most sad or vulnerable. What are you wearing? Are you happy, sad, angry, or scared? Are you able, as an adult, to hold the hand of your childlike self? Would you like to ask the child about their pain or confusion? You don't need to provide a remedy or solution, just listen.

When you are ready to speak, what does that child need to hear? Can you reassure the child, and tell them that it's not their fault? They are just doing the best they can. The adults in their life have their own problems, and it's not the child's fault. They are lovable just the way they are.

As you sit with the child, you are both covered in radiant light and energy. It is more beautiful and luminous than anything you have ever experienced. This is a guardian angel for both of you and you will always be protected and guided by this light.

Now, put your thumb and index finger together and think of a word and a color. In the future, when you put your thumb and index finger together again, the healing energy and light from right now will be with you.

You are coming back to the present moment, filling the room with your presence. You are safe, and secure. You are loved and accepted, and wonderful in every way.

Past Life Regression

I never believed in past lives until I experienced my clients going into their own past lives. For some, there is controversy on whether we can prove the existence of past lives. I currently believe that we have cellular memories from our ancestors that have been passed on to us. Based on those memories from our ancestors, we carry their trauma and karma that needs to be healed in this lifetime. To find freedom, we have to break away from our ancestral patterns that may be affecting us today. Not everyone will need past life regression, but it is an important component when working with abuse.

A Client's Past Life Regression Story

One day a client came to me who was struggling with her desire to share her wisdom and intuitive gifts. We went through the relaxation and she was drawn to a past-life memory in which her tongue was cut out, and her fingers chopped off when she spoke a truth that was unpopular and threatening to the tyranny in charge.

At the moment of death, she decided, "Don't tell the truth again". When asked how that could be altered safely five minutes before her painful and torturous execution, she shared, "Speak only the truth in a loving way. Don't be afraid, and fear will have no power over you."

Perhaps your memory is subtler, and may not even present itself in the moment. Remember that you're able to handle whatever situation occurs with loving detachment. You are surrounded with the prayer and protection of a powerful force that allows you to remember and be free. Take a moment to record your experience in your journal, even if it feels made up.

How Did These Processes Help Me?

The more I learned about hypnosis, past life regression, and working with my inner child, the more I was able to overcome my abuses by looking at them all from a different perspective. I was able to let go of my attachment to the negative emotions like anger, resentment, fear, guilt, and shame which I had attached to those events. Once I let go of all those negative emotions I started healing myself and finding freedom in my life. I changed my programing from victim to victorious.

In hypnosis, when you let go to the root cause, it doesn't hold you back any more. My favorite example has to do with taking Tylenol. When you take Tylenol, the pain goes away for six hours and then the pain comes back. You haven't taken care of the root cause of the problem or where it's coming from. In hypnosis you take care of the root cause of the issue, not bandage therapy, so you can move forward and be free of the abuse, event, or trauma that has been holding you back from living a purposeful life.

ACTION STEP: Balloon and Bucket Exercise
(Adapted from the work of Frank Garfield and Cheryl Bashada).
Test the power of your own mind.

Hold your arms in front of you, palms facing the ground.

Now close your eyes and breathe in slowly, allowing your shoulders to sink as you relax into a comfortable rhythm. Gently but firmly keep both arms raised, perpendicular to your body.

Imagine that in your left hand, you are carrying a heavy bucket, filled with water. Grasp the handle and hold the bucket at arm's length, resisting the pull of the heavy water, weighing it down.

Tied around your right wrist is a string, attached to a large, helium balloon. Feel how light your right arm is, and notice how the balloon floats through the air, getting lighter and lighter.

The left hand is struggling to resist the pull of the heavy bucket, growing heavier and heavier.

While the right hand is lifting, feeling lighter and lighter.

Now open your eyes and look at your hands. You will likely notice that one hand is significantly higher than the other.

You have just demonstrated the power of suggestion. Whatever your mind agrees with, your body responds to. So what image do you want to put in your mind today? Victim or victorious?

ACTION STEP: Inner Reflection through Self-Hypnosis

In a very real sense, all hypnosis is self-hypnosis, since you are in control of your thoughts and your mind. A skilled hypnotist can guide your thoughts to produce the brain wave state where you can be learning and change. They will then help you guide your mind by making carefully selected suggestions, based on their knowledge and training. But you can do some of this for yourself.

It is a great and wonderful skill to learn as it will enable you to use your powerful and wonderful mind to address anything which life can throw at you.

Just follow these simple steps.

First, make sure you are safe. If you are in your house run through the routine you would do if you were going out. Is the cooker turned off for example, is the door locked? Then make sure you will not be disturbed. Go into a room away from the family and turn your phone off.

Tell yourself that you are taking 20 minutes to work on helping yourself. It is your time and it is going to be enjoyable and rewarding.

Step One

Get comfortable and close your eyes. Starting with your feet and working your way to your head, tense and relax all the major muscle groups in your body.

Step Two

Breathe deeply, hold, let go.

Say to yourself: "I am twice as relaxed".

Repeat and say "more relaxed still".

Repeat this ten times.

Breathe normally.

Focus on breathing.

Feel the air going down into your lungs and your chest expanding.

Feel the tension leaving your body as you breathe out.

Each time say, "deeply relaxed".

Step Three

Notice the random thoughts in your mind.

Acknowledge each thought as it appears.

Let it drift away, watch it get smaller and smaller.

Say "come back later".

Repeat with next thought that comes.

Let your subconscious take over (at this time you may hear or see a kaleidoscope of images, enjoy them and regard them as an interesting creation which you have made).

Step Four

Imagine a safe place where you feel happy or secure. This may be a memory of a place you know or it can be somewhere you create in your imagination. Whichever feels right for you is the best.

Step Five

Imagine this place as strongly as you can, using all your senses.

Make the colors brighter and the picture clearer.

Listen for the sounds.

Feel the temperature.

Feel how the air or the ground feels on your body.

Notice the smells around you.

Step Six

Tell your mind to find any issue you wish to consider. Imagine you are holding it in your hand.

- Imagine it as an object in your hand.

- Now use your mind to change how that object looks and feels to you.

- Let any negative energy and connotations leave the object.

- Watch as they float away.

- Focus on the object as it changes and becomes what you want it to be. It is likely to feel lighter and look brighter.

- Turn it around in your hand noticing how the light reflects and refracts.

- Be aware that it is your powerful mind that is making these important changes.

- Let the changes happen, as they will, at the pace you choose.

- Continue until you know that you have done as much work as is right for you today.

- Put the object down but be assured you can return to do more work and make new discoveries if you want to.

- Focus on your safe and lovely place and notice any differences here.

- Promise your safe place that you will return very soon.

- Stretch out your arms and take a deep breath. Open your eyes and return to your everyday state.

Chapter 7 What Is the Role of Energy?

"Everything is energy, and that's all there is to it. Match the frequency of the reality you want, and you cannot help but get that reality. It can be no other way. This is not philosophy. This is physics."

- Albert Einstein

Everything is energy vibrating at its own frequency.

Energy cannot be created or destroyed, it can just change its pattern.

In this chapter, we are going to discuss three practices that help change the patterns of energy in your mind, body, and spirit. These are EFT, Reiki, and *chakra* balancing. Each help to release old and stuck energy in the body. It's important to learn about these because you can do the work in hypnosis and release your past, but energy from the events remains in your body at a cellular level. Healing requires that you dig deeper and go to that cellular level for total freedom. All three practices in this chapter release stuck energy trapped in the body.

The Body Is Made of Energy

We cannot see our body's energy, but we know it is there. Think of a computer. You cannot see the energy which is making it work, but you can see the results. If everything is working well, your computer loads quickly and the images on the screen look bright and clear. But if that energy is disrupted in some way then the computer locks up, or even crashes. The cause of the energy disruption needs to be identified and solved, then everything will work again.

Everything in the world is energy, including us. Of course, we are much more complex and wonderful than a computer, but the principle of free-flowing energy, and the harm which energy disruption can cause are the same.

Until recently, western medicine has tended to ignore the role of energy in how we work, although that is beginning to change. In the eastern traditions, the existence of energy and how it works in the body has been long established for thousands of years.

It is the foundation of acupuncture, acupressure, and emotional freedom techniques, all of which heal by working with the energy circuits, or meridians, of the body.

By using these techniques we can help energy flow freely throughout the body with an immense benefit to our emotional and our physical health. As the founder of EFT Gary Craig says, the cause of all negative emotions is the disruption of the body's energy system.

In rebalancing the system, we do not usually need to go into detailed traumatic memories, and that can feel very good for many clients.

How Are You Managing Your Energy?

Every thought, every emotion, and even every piece of furniture is emitting energy. Energy is impacting everything. That's why it's important to be choosy who we associate with and what we have in our homes.

I decided to become a Feng Shui practitioner to study the principles of this ancient Chinese practice of health, wealth, and relationships. I was frustrated with the difficulties my clients were having when they would go home and return to their former environment. They would lose all the good hard work they did during sessions.

Feng Shui is based on using energy force to harmonize individuals with their surroundings and environment. It uses the five elements: earth, wood, fire, water and metal, as well as the shapes of objects and their positioning, and the entire inner structure of the home (including different rooms, which represent different areas of your life.) The home and office function just like energy flow in the body: if the flow is interrupted, they don't work optimally.

You want your environment to be as stress free as possible. I taught my clients everything I knew about healing, but then they would return to a cluttered environment, thus leading them right back to their old energy patterns. When you declutter the inside, you must also declutter your outside environment as well. Feng Shui uses crystals, plants, cardinal directions and incense to create harmony in the environment.

Even after powerful three-day seminars on releasing and healing, clients were sucked back into the same habits when they return to a dysfunctional family or setting. Our environment has more power over us than we know, whether at home, at work, or with friends.

We're all connected. Either raising and praising one another, or disconnected by being judging and critical. Moment by moment we weave our reality. Sometimes we find that we have an energy vampire in our lives. When we leave them, we feel drained. Pay attention, and release them lovingly.

Healing With EFT

Emotional Freedom Technique was created in the United States by Gary Craig in the early 1990s. It's a process of tapping on your acupressure points to unlock stuck energy while you focus on an emotional judgment of a particular situation. You release the judgment through choosing to accept and forgive.

I first used EFT to manage my weight and stress. Now, I recommend it to my clients as a powerful and quick way to peel back layers that can accumulate around their hearts, restricting the flow.

At some point, I recognized I was covering up emotional layers of pain from my early abuse and suffering from addictive tendencies. What's addiction? I believe an addiction is a need for anything outside of ourselves that makes us feel good and free. My favorite addictions were to control, shop, perform for approval, and eat away my discomforts.

EFT is the tool I use before my hand reaches for the refrigerator. As I've tapped away layers of shame, anger, and resentment, I've found rejection, hurt, and betrayal underneath. It became less important to categorize them, but as I consistently tap them away, my authentic self is revealed.

I was always loved enough, adored, and safe. I had always possessed the power and the creativity I needed to succeed. But, it was only by removing the glaze on the clear vulnerability of my real self that I began to heal.

Perhaps you're aware of an emotion that's shut down deep inside. Like a vine, it's migrated from your thoughts and wrapped itself around your creativity, choking out your spontaneity. EFT is an amazing cordless trimmer that can whack it down to size.

Emotional energy isn't who you are. It's just passing through, like a weather system destined to shift. It only stays socked in, fogging your view, if you resist. EFT is based on accepting what's going on, and loving yourself and others anyway. Amazingly, acceptance clears you for takeoff for a higher point of view. One that's more inclusive and holistic.

As you tap various pressure points on your hands and face, the following affirmation is repeated each time: "Even though I have this fear, or other stuck emotion, I decide to love and accept myself completely." Not judging liberates you quickly. Acceptance is the ego's enemy. It's a magic potion that cures judging and dualistic thinking, which is an energy guaranteed to sour your days quickly.

As amazing as it might seem, our thinking minds create our reality. What we think about expands exponentially. The Mother, who dedicated her life to the work of Sri Aurobindo and the community at his ashram in Pondicherry, says, "Never think about a problem, it only strengthens it," When you say to yourself, "I decide to let it go," this moves the stuck energy out. This feels like relief. It is easy to see when I'm stuck, because the weather report is right inside, an invisible barometer that tells me what I'm seeing outside. This inside/outside paradox is uncanny in its accuracy.

When we check the weather report to see what to wear, it's sometimes accurate, and sometimes not. Our inside-out radar is more reliable. Letting go of stuck energy in motion, our *e-motion*, grants serenity.

Chakras: What They Are and Why They Matter

We have been talking of energy that is within us and in the world around us. Once we appreciate energy we can understand the importance of our seven main *chakras* (the Sanskrit word for wheel) for they are energy too. They are the points at which our mental, spiritual, and physical energies come together. They are the very fount of our being. It is worth us attending to them and looking after them as this can help us heal.

Each chakra is aligned to a major nerve center in the body. They interact as part of you and your constant energy flow. To work at optimal level, chakras need to be open, to move, and to balance. It is only then you have that free flow of energy through you that you have true wellbeing.

Life experience like abuse can harm this flow. You feel it in your body and soul.

A trauma or damaging memory can literally hurt your heart, affecting your fourth chakra. Anger recalled and unresolved can literally render you speechless, unable to speak your truth. This hurt may unbalance your fifth chakra, centered on your throat.

These hurts can damage your whole system, stopping your life's energy and weakening your spirit. Yet, you can reclaim your energy and rebalance your spirit. Honoring your feelings and acknowledging the work you need to do, you can heal.

Here is a brief description of the seven chakras, where they are located in your body, what they represent and how you will feel when they are in balance and your energy is flowing freely.

First Chakra: The *Muladhara*
Represents stability, security.
Located at the base of the spine.
When in balance you feel safe

Second Chakra: The *Svadhisthana*
Represents creativity, sexuality.
Located above the pubic bone.
When in balance you feel creative and free.

Third Chakra: The *Manipura*
Represents personal power.
Located from the navel to the breastbone.
When in balance you feel strong and in control.

Fourth Chakra: *The Anahata*
Represents the connection of mind, body, and spirit.
Located in the heart and chest.
When in balance you feel love, compassion, and kindness.

<u>Fifth Chakra</u>: The *Vishuddha*

Represents expression.

Located in the throat and mouth.

When in balance you easily and freely speak your truth.

<u>Sixth Chakra</u>: The *Ajna*

Located between the eyebrows.

Represents Intuition.

When in balance you have a deep knowledge that your life is being lived well for you.

<u>Seventh Chakra</u>: The *Sahaswara*

Located at the crown of the head.

When in balance you feel trust, true happiness at peace with yourself.

ACTION STEP: Affirmations

There are many powerful ways you can get balance back so your energy flows freely. This is often called balancing your *chakras*.

I have chosen affirmations because you will feel an immediate and powerful effect. With very little practice they are easy to do. Try for a few days and you will wonder how you ever lived without acknowledging this simple but powerful connection with your whole self.

First, reflect on where you feel uncomfortable and out of balance with yourself. Where in your body is that feeling located? How would you feel if you were in balance? Once you have identified which *chakra* you need to work on, choose the affirmation below. Remember it is *your* affirmation, adapt it for yourself. Then use it. Repeat it every day at least twice a day. Say it as often as you need. Dr. Wayne Dyer said that when we say anything after "I am…" you become the thing you believe that you are. Rather than become something negative, say what you are working toward or how you are recovering.

First Chakra

"I am growing into my own strength. My inner strength keeps me safe. With this safety, I can be brave."

Second Chakra

"I am full of ideas, wisdom, and pleasure. I can take this into the world."

Third Chakra

"I believe in my power. I love my strengths and accept my weaknesses. I can go into the world complete."

Fourth Chakra

"I feel warmth and love for those around me. I give and receive with my power."

Fifth Chakra

"My voice is within me. I take it to the world and speak clearly and strongly."

<u>Sixth Chakra</u>

"My life experience has given me wisdom. I use that wisdom in my love for others."

<u>Seventh Chakra</u>

"I am a wonderful, complete, and whole being. Every act I do reflects this truth."

How Do You Invest Your Energy?

Energy, like time and money, is a precious commodity. How you spend it creates your reality. What do you want to create in your life?

More drama? More conflict? Or peace and happiness? It's your choice.

It's a universal law that whatever you think about you bring about. What you focus on expands. As a nation, what are we focusing on? If we all focused on peace, there would be no more war. There would be no more suicide bombers.

Really, we're responsible for what we see. God doesn't create disharmony.

We're creating the water, the war, the unbalanced world that makes us all suffer. These are all consequences of our collective consciousness, our judging rather than loving mentality.

Even natural disasters are the result of mass consciousness. We're creating energy tsunamis. Our anger is heating up the planet with global climate change. Anger, hate, and war constitute the bleeding of the precious lives of Earth's beloved creations. The results are seen in every corner of our globe.

For instance, when someone asked Mother Theresa to come join an anti-war rally, she said, "I will come when you have a pro-peace rally."

What is Reiki?

In the process of healing myself, I became a Reiki master so that I could help other people heal. Reiki is a type of energy healing where a practitioners' hands are placed just above the body or even lightly touching the body. It can also be done long distance.

During a session, your Reiki practitioner works to channel universal life energy to you. The intention behind this is to reduce pain, increase relaxation, speed healing, and send energy directly to the physical and energetic parts of the body that need support.

Simply put, universal energy goes straight to the stuck and traumatized energy at the cellular level. You may feel lighter or liberated after, or simply deeply relaxed. You don't need to be consciously aware of how Reiki is working for it to have a deep impact on you. As a Reiki master, I use this energy with all my clients for added healing.

There's Cause and Effect

The ancient archery term *sin* meant shooting arrows or thoughts that didn't hit the target they were intended for. They're erratic, uncontrollable missed attempts. There's karma for our sins, our missing the mark. They aren't unforgivable, but are opportunities for us all to pick up the arrow and take aim again. Focusing only on the bulls-eye we want to nail.

Everything needs to be balanced. Even prayer can be excessive. Meditating in a cave isn't the walk of a spiritual master in today's world of need.

As spiritual beings, we can listen within for the answers, and go forth to serve.

When you pray to God, you give him your wish list. If it arrives, be grateful. If it doesn't, be patient. There's a divine lesson in everything. You're the chosen one, and you'll be blessed in any situation if you choose to receive the gifts and lessons that life is delivering. It is best to surrender and ask for Divine Will, rather than present an endless wish list to an imaginary Santa in the sky.

Forgiveness is payment in advance that blessings are arriving. Blessings cannot help but appear abundantly once you forgive. Just like physical open-heart surgery, when your heart is pure and open, things circulate beautifully.

ACTION STEP: A Simple EFT Routine

The great thing about EFT is that it is so simple to learn and to use. You use your fingers to tap on certain meridian points on your body while repeating powerful words. It is that simple! You can do it anywhere and you need no special equipment. Try it out and you will almost certainly feel better very quickly.

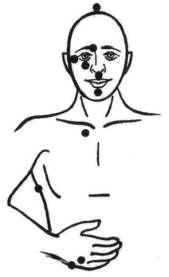

Even though I have this _____,
I completely accept myself, and choose
to let it go.

Say three times out loud while tapping on
the Karate Chop point on the side of the
hand. Follow the points in this picture.
Say your reminder phrase at every point.

Here is my guide to a quick self-help EFT routine:

1. Focus on the issue. EFT works best when you target one issue you
want to overcome. When you have decided on the issue, make a short

phrase which describes it for you, this will ensure you stay targeted in the session.

2. Focus on how the issue makes you feel and rate it on a scale, one for not too bad, ten for unbelievably awful. This is important as you will be able to chart your progress and see if the session makes you feel better.

3. Make an 'affirmation phrase'; a phrase which makes you feel powerful and able to deal with the issue.

4. Now put together the phrase which describes the issue and your powerful phrase in this form: "Even though (the issue) hurts me I will/I am (your powerful phrase)." Some people find it easier to use a form of words like: "I completely and deeply accept myself," for the affirmation phrase. If that feels right to you than do that.

The important thing is that you have a phrase which acknowledges the issue you want to deal with and a phrase which locks into your positive emotions and self-love.

Here are the points on which you should tap. Use your fingertips and tap gently but firmly. (You can use either side of the body and do not worry about being exact, it will work if you tap in the region of the meridian points).

- top of the head
- top of the eyebrows
- side of the eye
- under the eye
- under the nose

- under the chin

- under the collarbone

- under the arm

1. Tap seven times on each point while saying the phrase. Go around the points several (six to eight) times.

2. Stop and scale how you feel again on your one to ten scale. Almost certainly your pain will have gone down.

3. Decide if it is at a level which is comfortable for you. If you want to get the pain down some more then repeat the sequence.

It is that simple. There are other EFT routines which make the technique even more powerful. Google "EFT Gary Craig" and you will find a wealth of good information and You Tube videos which show you how it is done.

Chapter 8 Is There Freedom in Forgiveness?

"Our deepest fear is not that we are inadequate. Our deepest fear is that we are powerful beyond measure. It is our light, not our darkness that most frightens us. We ask ourselves, Who am I to be brilliant, gorgeous, talented, fabulous? Actually, who are you not to be? You are a child of God."

- Marianne Williamson

In the first few chapters we found what fears, thoughts and beliefs were holding us back from our stories.

So we start to reinvent ourselves. Then, using Hypnosis, NLP, EFT, and energy work, we begin to overcome our fears, and reprogram our mind and body. Now to find true freedom from the past we have to forgive and let go of all the people who have hurt us and harmed us.

When You Don't Forgive, You Relive

Dwelling on your past pain recreates the same negative energy in your body in the current moment. Your brain doesn't know that the event happened forty years ago. By thinking about it, it wells up all of the same toxic emotions, fear, and stress when, in reality, nothing is there.

You're hallucinating a terrifying scene. You're sitting in the safety of your living room, reliving the anxiety and misperceptions of an old drama.

There are new virtual reality machines on the market that activate a variety of emotions. People sit in a chair, and erupt in erratic, terrified, blissful, weepy, and surprised ways behind their video masks. This is a powerful example of what we're unconsciously doing all day long, with unintended powerful results. We are replaying our own virtual reality programs that we have embedded in our minds. It's time to take off our masks and face reality.

Forgiveness clears our path moving forward. It's what you need to reconnect with the Divine. If you focus on what should have been instead of accepting what is, you miss the life lessons in freedom. Forgiveness shifts undesired energetic replays over and over again.

The Journey From Fear to Freedom is Filled With Forgiveness

I believed my mother was never there for me. I thought that she favored her sons before me, which was my never-good-enough self-fulfilling prophecy. When she died, all of her sons were present to say goodbye, while I was out of the country and couldn't be present at her death bed.

I had no chance to say goodbye and have closure. I was angry and felt again that I wasn't good enough because she couldn't wait for me. I wasn't important enough to wait for to say goodbye.

Thank God for my holistic friends or I couldn't have healed this time. Joanne Edwards held an *Adventure in Excellence,* a three-day workshop that presented a different perspective; another way to see my relationship with my mom. Joanne role played as my mother in the seminar where I could say everything I ever wanted to say to my mom and forgave her for leaving me without saying good bye.

Joanne pointed out that it wasn't that mom didn't love me, or that I wasn't as important as the boys. It was that she loved me so much that if I had been present, it would have been too hard for her to go, to leave her baby behind.

When I considered this, I felt a completion that I'd never known. It melted me. Finally, I realized that I had always been precious and loved by my mother. I also realized that our relationship never ends. I can feel an intimate love now. I can feel a love that she couldn't fully express before, because it wasn't taught to her. I now believe that she loved me the most.

Every Human Contains the Capacity to be Whole-hearted, Loved, and Complete

I came to realize that forgiveness wasn't about letting another person off the hook. It was about releasing my bondage to something that offended me deeply. As long as I held the perception that they had wronged me, I was stuck in that offensive space and couldn't release it.

The bondage to drama was always completely in my capacity to drop. Like a tug of war ends when I let go of the resistance on my end of the rope. The dis-ease that I was feeling owned me, literally making me ill.

Through this ongoing lack of ability to appreciate the sweetness in my life, I manifested diabetes. Diabetics cannot absorb sugar, so it gets dumped into the bloodstream, causing blood sugar levels to spike. It causes a roller coaster, up and down insulin ride, representing the inability to love and be loved. Just like riding a roller coaster, I was feeling sick to my stomach.

I have learned to slow down and reconnect with the divine within me and all around me. My blood absorbs life's sweetness and my experience becomes smoother.

I Grew Up Believing in a Spiritual Presence

An important message in the Holy Quran is "He who finds himself, finds God".

As I let go of my layers to find my true loving self, I found God.

I have always believed in a force that's helping us and with us all the time. Now I have come to call it God, the Divine, or Universe. I didn't tap into it as much in my early life as I do today.

About ten years ago, my call for higher consciousness went out, and I began to attract different teachers to help me on the path. Lao Tzu said, "When the student is ready, the teacher will appear."

I was ready.

How to Forgive the Unforgivable

I see the world with new eyes. I forgave the boy, I forgave the chauffeur. I forgave the *molana* by role playing and writing forgiveness letters. I realized in my mind and body that I was carrying resentment and poisoning myself which was not serving my purpose in life to be a healer.

The other NLP technique I used was to look at each event in my life as an observer from above. I was detached from the scene and the emotions. Only then I could forgive each and every one of them and learn the lessons they brought. They became my teachers. If those traumatic events hadn't happened, I wouldn't have worked on myself and found my true love and freedom.

I also wrote letters of forgiveness to each of them and released them to the Divine in order to love myself and them.

ACTION STEP: Forgiveness

Get your journal. One by one, write a letter to each and every one who has hurt you. And say everything you ever wanted to say to them and couldn't. Use this letter to forgive them for all the hurt and abuse and release it by burning it on full moon.

ACTION STEP: An NLP Technique for Forgiveness

The discipline of Neuro Linguistic Programming can be a wonderful tool in helping us to forgive past hurts. It is a discipline which enables us to change how we process our thoughts and feelings so they no longer hurt us but serve and help us.

Try this thought experiment and notice how your feelings have changed afterwards.

- Identify a person who had hurt you and where you feel this hurt is still doing you harm.

- Take a moment to think about that person and how you feel about it now. If you feel it is time for you to forgive this person do the following:

- Get a picture of that person in your mind.

- Now think about a person who harmed you, who you have forgiven because you recognized that they had done the best that they could at the time (perhaps a young person or a child)

Picture Each Person Side By Side

- Notice the differences between the two. Here are some of the things you might see:
    - Brightness (is one person brighter in your picture?)
    - Colours
    - Location (is one person closer to you in the picture?)
    - Sounds each make

Then try to switch the people around. Swap their positions. Notice how that feels different.

After you have completed this exercise, you may find that the person you struggled to forgive no longer holds such an emotional charge for you.

STEP THREE:
REINFORCE

Chapter 9 Is Love the Answer?

*"Your **beliefs** become your thoughts*
*Your **thoughts** become your words*
*Your **words** become your actions*
*Your **actions** become your values*
*Your **values** become your destiny."*

--Mahatma Gandhi

Beginning to Love Myself

Now that we have reinvented our self in the first step by finding out our stories and beliefs we took on from our past experiences than reprogramed our beliefs in the second step
Using Hypnosis, EFT, NLP and energy work, we can now reinforce our daily new thoughts and perception of our self to make it concrete in our mind. It takes 40 days to make or break a new habit in my experience so that's why I do six sessions with my clients so they can create the new habits and lifestyle full of love and freedom,.

Loving me has made all the difference. I know it sounds like 1960's flower power, but it's an even better trip than psychedelics. Falling in love with me feels groovy.

Words can't convey the feeling of liberation that I feel when I look in the mirror and I like who is looking back at me. It is a delightful adventure, a discovery of new lessons I'm creating, and new people I'm attracting that teach me about how delightful and lovable I can be. The moment I accept that *I'm the goofball,* things get delightfully funny and wonderful again. When I started loving and accepting myself, everything shifted in my life; my relationship, my health and my wealth. It's a domino effect. Whatever the state of mind you are in, it affects every area of your life. Look up these two excellent self-help books that are relevant to this chapter:

"*Wherever You Go, There You Are,*" by Jon Kabat Zinn

"*Loving What Is,*" by Byron Katie

It's never too late to have a happy childhood. We're the directors of the movie, so we can change the story any time. Then we get to review it and decide how long it plays. It's always your choice to be in fear or freedom.

How to Love

How do we learn to come from a space of love regardless of the situation we're in or the negativity of people we see? We all have a difficult person we might prefer not to be seated next to at a dinner party. No matter the level of difficulty, we can find love in anyone. We're all created by the same Source. These situations flex our spiritual muscles, sculpting strength and consistent capacity.

There are no bad people, just bad behaviors. The Lord didn't create anyone to be bad. They'll suffer the consequences of their bad behavior all on their own. The Universe takes care of it. It's not our responsibility to punish them or suffer needlessly in our own mind.

I heard a story once that deeply impressed me, about a woman who forgave and took her son's killer into her home. She used the power of her free-will choice divinely. She chose to see the unity of them, the divine lesson of their situation. She saw that she could create the possibility of a loving relationship with a person who had killed her only son. The bottom line is: no matter what the struggle is, the answer will be coming from love.

We Get to Choose

We can all create new possibilities in our lives if we choose to. Each moment gives us a crossroads from which to choose. Are we loving ourselves and others? Or are we creating lonely walls?

Once I decided that I had a choice in every situation good, bad, right, or wrong I found my peace and freedom. A lot of people live in regret, needlessly torturing themselves.

"I could have." "I would have." "I should have."

Life is a learning laboratory. When we go to school, we're taught a lesson, and then tested. Life works differently. First, it delivers the test, and then gives us the opportunity to learn the lesson.

When the student is ready, the teacher will appear. When the student is truly ready, the teacher will disappear." — Lao Tzu

I feel that the Divine keeps testing us until we learn the lesson. Then we move on to the next lesson or course. The sooner we learn it, the quicker we find freedom. It's all about learning to let go and let God. When we really master a certain subject or situation, we graduate and are no longer tried in that way.

If we're focused on letting go and letting God, things fall into place. Recently, I had an argument with my husband. It's not clear what the disconnect was about. Something to do with directions and driving, a classic husband and wife dispute. I was getting really righteous and my ego was in the way. Then I found myself change my own mental direction and thought, "Okay, what would God do in this situation? Let go of the ego."

When I ask that question, I immediately go from fearful to free. That's the ticket to freedom for me. It diffused the situation immediately. There was no more argument. The disconnect which had been created in my perception was healed at the root of its source, and the outer manifestation shifted immediately.

According to Albert Mehrabian, ninety-three percent of all communication is nonverbal. People feel our positions intuitively through our tone and body language, and respond accordingly. Are we talking down to them or exalting them? Celebrating their brilliance or chastising their mistakes?

This is so simplistic and yet incredibly powerful and easy in every situation. Whatever the problem, the solution is coming from a place of love.

Being Present with Detachment

Relationships effect everything in life. If you don't have a loving, peaceful relationship in your life, the rest doesn't come easy. If you're not happy at home, you can't be happy at work. As I've learned about my blind spots, healed my relationships with my family and others, and learned to be loving not judging, I've been able to connect more with the Divine.

When I did Landmark Education (see more on this in the resources section), I thought I knew everything. But what I learned was that I still had blind spots that I was not aware of. The story that I made up about myself after the sexual abuse had nothing to do with the abuse. Because events happen in our lives, good or bad, what we tell ourselves after the event is our choice. We can choose to be in fear, or in freedom, the choice is yours. The bottom line is stop judging and start loving your life. If you don't resolve your past, it still plays in the background and you don't even know it. I learned about being in the moment. At first, I didn't know what being in the moment meant. People talked about it a lot, but how do you really get there?

I didn't understand for the longest time why that would help me. So what if I don't have a perfect relationship with a sibling? What does that have to do with me now? How can you have perfect relationships with everyone anyway?

Teaching other clients has helped me to understand this, I realized that I'm sharing the journey within, including awareness, being present, and completing with people in your life with whom you have been incomplete. It became clear to me that this was being in the moment.

I've learned it's not about creating a perfect relationship, it's about being in a peaceful place with whatever is happening and coming from love and nothing. At first, I didn't know what love and *nothing* meant.

It's my understanding that when we come from nothing, we're detached from the outcomes and come from love only, accepting what is. When we talk about being, it's a difficult idea to get. I teach the five love languages, relationship bank accounts, and personality styles and preferences. All of which give some concrete tools and ways to shift from fear to freedom. Ultimately, the big 'Ah-Ha' is that it's all about us, not them. When we change, others change around us. When we try to change them, they resist. The irony is that when you change yourself, people around you shift.

Recently, all of the lessons I was getting had to do with being, which I learned happens at a soul level. Being on a soul level in the presence of an unconditionally loving person, you feel them before they even open their mouths. Their very presence is transformative. One feels drawn to their presence automatically in the Divine Work. They're easy to be with and feel accepted.

That's really what Christ and all of the prophets practiced: being unconditionally loving. Coming from the nothingness creates a space for everything. When there's nothing, you can create anything. It's the powerful feminine void of creativity. I keep the following quote on the wall of my kitchen:

"When nothing is certain, everything is possible."

It's a good quote for a kitchen where you create things to eat.

This is the time when we're all becoming Christ-like or raising our Krishna, Buddha, or Mohammad Consciousness. They talked about raising consciousness. But what's the difference between raising our consciousness and accessing the subconscious, which is ninety percent of us, I wondered?

When you're 100% present, you're in a higher state of consciousness. Everything is happening at the same time, aligning love, past, present, and future; anything is possible. When we raise our consciousness, we're living in loving oneness with Divine

Everything is now; it's not in the past or future, as Eckhart Tolle says in the *Power of Now*. There's no then or yet to be, it's all right in this instant. Every instant in which you arrive fully in the moment transforms you from the illusion of three-dimensional reality into the reality of the infinity of timeless time.

The two resources that transformed my life as well are *The Power of intention* and *Divine Love,* by Wayne Dyer. One taught me that everything starts with intention and the other taught me that it is all love and the rest is illusion. Please consider them transformation gifts for your journey.

The Stairway to Heaven is a Lifelong Journey

I realize that my master teacher is my husband, Nasir – the one with whom I struggle the most. Without him, I wouldn't have worked so hard finding my Self, my peace, and my own identity.

I'm eternally grateful to him for being who he is, a very kind, understanding, and loving man. Now, when we communicate, we respond to one another's authentic self, instead of reacting to one another's idiosyncrasies, and that has made all the difference. Every Friday we do date night celebrating our new love.

Each step in my evolution of consciousness was made possible by rising higher and leaving behind a lower state of consciousness, whether a belief, heaviness, grievance, or resentment. And it was a gradual process that spiraled around to the same issues but at higher and higher perspectives, like a spiral staircase. What was happening at a psychological level was also happening on the physical in the spiraling crystalline composition of my DNA strands. These evolving RNA/DNA strands are actually shifting from a physical human self to a new, divine, fully conscious Self. It's like an energetic stem cell infusion from the Divine.

My traditional Muslim teachings were by the Prophet, who had gone into the desert for meditation where he received divine messages from God. As I learned Christian/American traditions, I noticed the same truths in the Koran and Bible stories.

I Realized that Buddha's, Krishna's and Jesus' Stories Were My Story

This same story lives within you. A story of all living beings growing toward the light and raising consciousness. An alchemical transmutation in your cells, which elevates you from merely human to a divine being, according to The Mother and Sri Aurobindo's Integral

Yoga (a form of Yoga which enables us to open up to the Divine Power within us). In the process of climbing my stairway to spirituality I became a yoga and meditation instructor too.

As incredible as this may seem, it's really a scientific outcome of each human being's progression through the life lessons that come from human experience over many lifetimes.

These things are my destiny revealing itself. It's a beautiful and honorable journey, bringing great joy and celebration to my days. I'm honored to be of service in assisting others on their path, and fulfilled by my own soul's destiny in learning to become an enlightened leader of human evolution into fully conscious Spiritual Oneness.

I make it a part of my daily ritual to pray five times. First, I wash my hands, feet, and face, preparing for the inner cleansing of my being to receive God. The tender transformation of my being from judging to loving always arrives. It's something I have become sure of on a cellular level, and that has made all of the difference in my life. In my experience making the intention to change is the most important step followed by action. Knowledge followed by action is the key to success.

A Pool of Consciousness

Awareness of society's negativity surrounding us is the beginning of a path to liberation and freedom. We appear to be individual beings on earth, but in reality, we're One. Slowing down and tapping into our sixth, intuitive sense, our thoughts become more conscious.

To recap, becoming self-aware is the first step to liberation and freedom, so what stops us from taking on this responsibility? It's our fear of moving out of our comfort zone. We're bombarded with unwanted thoughts and feelings. Remember, they are not our own, FEAR is really *False Evidence Appearing as Reality*. We transcend fear by filtering emotions, and then re-view the thoughts that created them, then we change and consciously create with them again. We're the pivot points in the change we seek.

Our minds are blank tablets and we're their scribes. Our thoughts literally write the scripts of our lives. The things that we believe, we become while we live.

Removing ideas imposed on us from a fearful family or society stops sowing the same seeds that grow into weeds where we get stuck in ruts. Our capacity to co-create, and freedom to choose consciously, is the mark of an evolving soul; an exalted example for mankind's evolution.

Slowing down, I find that the grinding gears of my habitual thinking requires great commitment and courage to choose. It's a constant surrendering, handing over the reins of my mind to Divine Mind. I pause and realize, "I don't know what to write here, on this blank page of a new day, but You do." A surrendered simple request opens the faucet for the Divine to intercede: "Please teach me, inspire me, and work through me".

Awakening and inquiring, "What would you have me do? How shall I proceed?" delivers the keys that opens doors to the spiritual kingdom. Then the energy manifestation arrives just when we need it in divine time. Doors are opened for us before we even arrive, and we're given the lines of what to say, to whom, and at the right time.

Intuition Is Our Inner Truth and Guidance

To tap into our intuition, we have to start with the intention first. In the process of taking the next step in my spiritual journey, I took a one-year course with Lori Lipton in order to learn how to incorporate intuitive mastery into my work. Lori is a psychic, shaman, medium, and healer. My awakening to love and intuitive guidance was not overnight. I did a great deal of work to get where I am. I've learned to tap into my intuitive higher self easily through my daily meditations.

No matter what you struggle with, if you can learn the practice of two, you will receive the healing you seek. **Two minutes of prayer, two minutes of journaling, two minutes of meditation**, and the answers will come.

Intuition is the key to unlocking the doors we long to open. It taps into the ninety percent of us that knows what's best for us, heart, and mind. Learning to listen to my intuition has been a process for me, first hearing, and then trusting my inner voice.

We all have this inner voice that tells us what's best for us. Often, we're too busy with worldly activities to listen. We ignore our intuition even if we hear it. The art of living life authentically is learning to hear and then choosing to act consistently and intuitively.

Sometimes, I'm so busy chasing my tail that I forget to listen to myself and others. I'm so busy running from one task to the other, doing what I think I need to be doing to get where I should be, that

I'm checked out. I think I'm accomplishing a lot, but I'm absent, off-center, and repeat the same thing over and over expecting different results. "Insanity is repeating the same mistakes and expecting different results" (Alcoholics Anonymous, *The Big Book*, 1979).

Finally, I discovered a power tool for getting unstuck: softening my ego mind with the grace of Divine mind. It's called meditation. Lifting our human experience to see it as God does; as if already perfect. Interestingly it's only one letter different from mediation. It invites a peaceful resolution space for grace to arrive.

When I met Ashwin Kapadia of Savitri Mission, he made it very simple. Meditation is just sitting still for two minutes at a time. That's it, and breathing. I realized I could easily insert that into my daily practice.

Every day after my prayers, I sit still for two minutes. In prayer, I talk to God. In meditation, God answers me. If I'm still and present, I receive Divine presents and presence.

My new stretch goal is to remember to meditate two minutes every two hours without setting a timer. This is my most recent learning and remembering to do so will be rewarding.

Surrender

Before, going to funerals was very hard for me because of my fear of death. Now I have realized that the soul never dies we just transfer from this world to the next.

Recently, I watched a close friend bury her thirty-year-old son. I don't recall the words the *molana* spoke, but still deeply feel her grief as the casket was lowered beneath her feet. Ashes to ashes, dust to dust. To whom we came from, we shall return. We all will go through this life cycle of birth, growth, death, and then back again to the Oneness.

Many events, remarkable and small, defy comfort or understanding. How can we possibly accept responsibility for creating such suffering and tragedy in our world? Despite our deepest desires, life sometimes delivers tragedies that can only be endured by surrendering, giving ourselves up to a higher power, to let go and let God.

Words are powerless in the face of such heartbreak and ruin. Loss of loved ones, dignity, control, wealth, and freedom sometimes seems impossible to bear. As we beat our heads against the wall, and hold our bloodied heart in our hands, sometimes, we can only ask for a help that we desperately need yet barely believe in.

Once called, the Mother of us all cannot help but arrive. She has never been gone, it was only that our perception was skewed. Asking humbly to be led because we don't know another way, we begin to be shown a new way.

It may appear ugly, impossible, or undesirable. Yet, somehow, when we begin to let go, the light within us molds us and makes this impossible path our passion. Much after our wounds have begun to heal, we begin to see the wisdom of the most excruciating lessons life delivers. Living through a pain that blinds us, we begin to see differently: compassionately and courageously through the heart.

Deciding to lean into, rather than run from, our demons transforms them into allies and friends on our vision quest. Accepting this part of us makes us whole and complete, and to resist our shadow side only makes it persist.

As We Were Editing This Book, I Became Mute

Like an orange-beaked mute swan, when I opened my mouth, nothing came out. At first, I thought it was just a cold or laryngitis, and that it would pass. Then the days became a week, and I realized that my healing mantras and meditations and prayers weren't powerful enough, as they usually were, to clear the situation. I went to a specialist, who informed me that there was a node along my vocal chords that had literally stretched the tender tissue so taut that a hole had emerged. This hole kept the breath from passing along the tuning fork of my vocal chords, and only a painful raspy whisper could be heard.

My belief in healing spontaneously is strong, yet I'm also grounded in reality, and I eventually yielded to surgery. I now realize that the quiet that ensued during this six-week healing process caused me to surrender and center in a way that I had never found possible with my hectic schedule and social life.

Slowing down and taking time to quiet my mind connects me with my Higher Self. Scattered multitasking abdicates divine guidance for ego supremacy. We think we're getting ahead in our world when we're really missing the boat.

Soon, all of the very important tasks and visiting times were silenced, and I began even more to accept that all this was divine, and I was along for the perfect ride. I released the need to push for a deadline. I had hit a wall, and began to surrender and accept the divine timing for the perfect outcomes I needed.

Words are not adequate to express the bliss that I began to feel in the simplicity of my days. The prayers I gave five times a day to Mecca and the presence of the Prophet began to blend. The whole day, my whole home, my whole family, and all of my friends praying for me became a sacred mat upon which I placed my head in deep respect.

Certainly, there were times of stress, and my agenda wasn't kept. Yet, *the* agenda, Mother's plan, was unfolding in ways that I could never have arranged if I had continued to try to control it. Quite simply, it became a shift from my power and my will to Divine power and grace.

Even now, I'm in awe at the speed with which I healed, remarkable according to my surgery specialist. I wasn't the healer but the healed, and as I let go of layer after layer of resistance, the essence of my true empowerment began to emerge. It didn't happen suddenly, but spontaneously. It wasn't something that I could force; I had to yield. It seemed to have had its own personal experience of what Dr. David Hawkins wrote about in his book, *Power vs. Force*. He speaks about the measurability of consciousness and our capacity to transcend our force, or ego consciousness, through practice, surrender, and meditation.

Great mystics and healers say, as they emerge from a trauma that demanded all that they had, that ripping the fiber of their previous selves so a more expansive and magnificent new Self could arrive was a great gift.

I'm almost reluctant, as absurd as it seems, to speak again. Silence has become a sacred solace in which I'm surrounded by bliss in a way that I've never experienced. Listening is really an act of God. By listening, we go into presence and connect to our highest more Divine self. Brilliance doesn't need to speak; it just needs to be.

One other thing is certain: each moment of bliss is followed by another moment of blessing, sometimes veiled as an unwanted challenge. The more powerful the challenge, the greater the grace and bliss that rewards us when we have surrendered it completely. There's nothing that I'm asked to do on my own. I came from the bliss that loves me without exception or reason. It's to that presence, that eternal loving Mother of my essence, that I now take every situation and circumstance with which I'm presented.

It used to be that I would only "bother" Her when it was something I couldn't master on my own. Now I'm beginning to realize that each breath is a surrender, a giving up of what has been, so that which is present can be offered to her presence to transform. This is my role as a woman of the twenty-first century. I now live a happy, successful life, married for 35 years. I have faced my fears one by one, and released them to the divine. I now know that everything starts with an intention, intention turns into the impulse to take action, and action results in a life of freedom, filled with love.

Shoulder by shoulder we stand as sentries, stepping down the essential reality that we may have only glimpsed in our dreams. Alone we're not able, but together, we're invincible. I dedicate this day, and all days that the sun will dawn upon us all to you, invincible one. I believe in you. I believe in us. Together, we're victorious!

ACTION STEP: Questions became my quest

Explore these questions in your journal:

Do you love yourself?

Do you love others unconditionally?

Who can you reach out today to acknowledge your
Love for them?

What are you thankful for today?

Does your life matter?

Do you make a difference in the world?

What legacy do you want to leave?

ACTION STEP: Candle Light Meditation

Adapted from Eva Wilson

1. Begin with an unlit candle in front of you.

2. Take a deep breath and close your eyes.

3. Relax and leave behind all concerns as you breathe out.

4. Give yourself a gentle hug inside and remind yourself you are loveable just the way you are.

Now open your eyes and light the candle while holding this intention: quietly observe the candlelight as it represents

Unconditional love. All worldly worries are leaving your mind and body as you breathe out. Enjoying love and light, replacing those worries.

The candlelight is a reflection of your own heart light. Which is your heart chakra. This is your inner master and the god light within you. Feel the wholeness and peace inside.

Now as you blow the candle out, continue to carry this light in your heart, full of love all day. Repeat each day.

ACTION STEP: The Four Agreements

"The Four Agreements," by Don Miguel Ruiz, is a must-read book for everyone. It is empowering if you take it seriously and keep these four simple agreements with yourself.

1. **Be impeccable with your word** because you *are* your word. Words have meaning, and whatever you say or how you describe anything in life, is how you feel about it. When you use words that are not conducive to your goal, it takes you away from your goal. Use empowering words in your conversations to free yourself and others.

2. **Don't take anything personally**. I used to take everything my husband said personally and make it about me. This hurt our relationship tremendously. Once I stopped doing that, my relationship shifted from fear to freedom.

3. **Don't Assume Anything**. When you assume, you make an ass out of you and me.

4. **Do Your Best**. As long as you do your best in every situation, you will not live in regret.

I have been practicing all four agreements in my own journey, and I am still in the process of mastering them.

Chapter 10 Being of Service

"The best way to find yourself, is to lose yourself in the service of others."
- Mahatma Gandhi

One of the greatest gifts that I have learned is to give and receive at the same time, allowing God's work to flow through me to those in need.

The reasons for telling my life story, including the long-term effects of being touched inappropriately, were not clear to me for some time. It has called me to an unexpected act of service.

Nine years ago, I joined PWAM (Pakistani Women's Association of Michigan) to help women in my community through education, empowerment, and assistance. When I was asked to be a founding member and the general secretary of the organization, it felt like it was my calling.

We have done a lot of charity work since then. Recently, a Pakistani woman was kicked out of her home by her husband. We found her a place to stay and supported her with a safe space. We have also volunteered with soup kitchens. I loved taking food to the poor people in Detroit for breaking the Ramadan fast. It's so fulfilling feeding them good food.

We hold an annual community bazaar for community women to sell their food, clothes, and jewelry. It's a joyful celebration of creativity meeting needs. We give an annual woman of the year award to honor exceptional serving. We're the first Pakistani women's organization registered in the country. We were thrilled when Michigan State Senator Debbie Stabenow came to our event, recognizing and encouraging us. We were honored by the Pakistani Ambassador in Washington, DC, who sent the first check to help sponsor our safe house. Honestly, this is one of the most fulfilling things I've ever been a part of!

This gift from our community takes care of physically, sexually, and mentally abused women by buying a safe house for women. We get calls from women who are emotionally or sexually abused and are kicked out of their homes. We want women to have a space where they can find refuge from the abuse that they're suffering from without the angst of fleeing.

This organization provides the ability to meet women's immediate physical needs. Then, we provide them with workshops to educate and empower them. We have qualified counselors, social workers, and physicians to treat their needs.

In authentic Islam, women have a lot of power and respect. Women in Iran are taxi drivers, pilots, and soldiers, able to do anything, contrary to the media depiction of them being cloistered.

Culturally, Muslims living in Michigan are liberated. There's no submission, and the abuse issues are the same ones that Christian women face. However, abuse in Muslim families tends to be hidden behind closed doors. Nobody talks about until it gets really bad.

My mission is to talk about it safely. In revealing it, we begin to heal it. We offer women tools and resources that end suffering and lonely misery. I want every woman to know that there's only one degree of separation between us. You don't have to suffer alone in silence anymore. You can heal in your own mind using the 3 steps in the book.

Now it's Your Turn

Please use the resources in this book to begin to shift your story. I did it with support, and you can too. If a resource that I've shared calls to you, take time to go to the library or a bookstore to begin your own journey to freedom.

Remember the three stages of my journey and use them in your own. Just having finished reading this book means you have started the reinvention stage. Take a close look at your stories, your history of abuse, and how you are perpetuating the drama in your own life.

After you have gained some awareness into how your past is affecting your present, you're moving into the reprogramming stage. This is when you utilize your resources to overcome your limiting beliefs and decisions that have kept you stuck. If it is helpful, use hypnosis, EFT, or NLP work as I did.

After that, the third stage is to reinforce the healing work you have done. Look for the love that exists in your life, look for ways to be more loving, incorporate loving practice into your everyday thoughts and actions. Use your new tools to reinforce your new habits. This is how you become the new you. Free from your past.

Remember too that no matter what your issue, I deeply believe that the answer lies in meditation. It's not as complicated as your ego makes it out to be. Just be present no matter what you are doing. For me, meditation is not just sitting quietly for 2 minute, it is having tea each day with my 92 year old father-in-law. Meditation is working with my clients. It is cooking for my family. It is in everything that I do.

Be present to the moment and watch how effortlessly you move from fear to freedom. Now that you have the knowledge you must take daily actions towards your goal.

ACTION STEP: Daily Practices reinforced.

When I wake up in the morning, I wake up in gratitude for my health, wealth, and relationships. I ask God to protect my house and my kids. I ask God to give me the ability to serve mankind. I start out every morning and say all of this before my feet hit the floor.

I ask God and my higher resources to help me stick to my goals today. I'm not beating myself up for where I was yesterday, but focused in this moment on the direction I want to go; the present of a new day.

People say practice makes perfect, I say perfect practices make perfect. This is the key to success.

Commit to the following every day:

- Deep breathing, two minutes
- Tapping (EFT), two minutes
- Meditation (quiet your mind), two minutes
- Visualization (perfect image of you), two minutes
- Journaling, two minutes
- Self-hypnosis two minutes

Afterword

Dear Reader,

I first met Hena Husain at a past life workshop at her office in Southeast Michigan. I was immediately drawn to her generosity and eagerness to learn, coupled with a strong desire to serve.

I learned more about Hena as I worked with her in various capacities. She was my hypnotherapist, we studied together in Savitri Mission with the Mother and Sri Aurobindo's work, and we told our common stories and peeled back the layers together of shared protection mechanisms.

She lived in Pakistan when I lived in Somalia. We both experienced molestations at the age of seven, shared the turmoil of moving around the world to new cultures, and skipping second grade because we were bright for our age.

Hena's remarkable journey probably mirrors your own story in uncanny, amazing ways. She is the brave and vulnerable being that is bringing this #MeToo movement into her vast heart with the grace of the Universal Mother for us to heal.

Not just to report the shameful episodes and experiences, but to give us a guidebook on how to begin the process of healing and transforming these experiences into our greatest gifts and strengths. As we move beyond our unspoken horrors, we reunite with the truth of our innocence and freedom.

This book shifts our loneliness and separation into the common ballroom of empowering the feminine within all women, men, and children. The sacred self that longs to be heard, held, and witnessed as it reclaims its essential innocence again. This work is a global gift that transcends the Muslim and Christian cultures. Both sides will feel comfortable in her story, honored and compassionate for the other as they read and feel the truth of our common experiences.

This is the bridge that will liberate us from the three-dimensional illusion that we are lack beings and wounded in ways which make us unlovable. Together our healing and love will build the bridges which will expand beyond physical boundaries to bridge the global space of healing and peace.

As we embrace the peace within ourselves, we will begin to see the mirrored peace of our outer reality emerge. We are as one alone, only a flicker of light Divine. Together, we are the light of the world igniting as we move toward a new golden age which is emerging.

I am a Christian woman who bows to the vast compassion and kindness of the Muslim women who have welcomed me into their *sad* celebrations, wedding festivities, and sacred healing circles. I have been honored to learn that the Lord Jesus Christ is revered in the Holy Book of the *Koran*, and I open my heart with you to discover the oneness of our faith and the common family of our grace. May we heal ourselves and so heal the world.

If you are moved by this work and wish to make a difference, please consider contributing to the safe space in Southeast Michigan for women who have fled abuse and need help for themselves and their children. A dollar from the proceeds of each book you buy goes to this mission. Consider buying copies for your loved ones, school, and community libraries.

We are also deeply grateful for one time or monthly donations to:

www.BalanceForLife.com
Pakistani Women's Association of Michigan (PWAM)
PO Box 8888
Southfield, MI 01010-1111

May thanks be to God, the Common Uniter of all living beings.

Gratefully,
Ellen Waara
President
Inside Solutions, Inc.

RECOMMENDED READING LIST

Now that your journey is well under way, here are some more life changing books to reveal what else is possible:

The Four Agreements by Don Miguel Ruiz

Supreme Mastery of Fear by Joseph Murphy

The Biology of Belief by Bruce Lipton

The Power of Intention by Wayne Dyer

A Course in Miracles by Helen Schucman

The 5 Love Languages by Gary Chapman

You Can Be Happy No Matter What by Richard Carlson

49 Life Lessons it took me 50 years to learn by Jennifer Forster

The Tapping Solution by Nick Ortner

What I Know for Sure by Oprah Winfrey

Divine Love by Deepak Chopra

Wherever You Go, There You Are by Jon Kabat Zinn

Loving What Is by Byron Katie

RECOMMENDED COURSES

The Landmark Forum www.landmarkworldwide.com

Adventures in Excellence by Joanne Edwards

A Short Guide to Three Types of Helpful Therapy

Hypnosis

"The American Psychological Association defines hypnosis as "A state of consciousness involving focused attention and reduced peripheral awareness characterized by an enhanced capacity for response to suggestion."

It is a very good way to change beliefs and behaviors which are no longer helpful to you.

Hypnosis is a very gentle and natural therapy which uses your natural 'trance' states to work with your unconscious mind to make the changes you would like. You will know these states yourself, when you are day-dreaming, for example, or you are deeply concentrating.

A skilled hypnotherapist can create this state and then use it to uncover memories, thoughts, and emotions which may be hurting you or blocking your development. They will also use the positive memories and resources you bring, so you will be directed to use your own very powerful mind to help yourself.

It is important that you choose a recognized and expert practitioner. Make sure they are properly insured and registered with a reputable professional organization.

If you go to my website

http://www.balanceforlife.biz/about.php, you can see the organizations which I belong to. If you cannot get to see me, I would advise you choose a therapist who is a member of a similar organization.

Neuro Linguistic Programming

NLP begins with the knowledge that at any time we only perceive a small part of our world. Our perception is filtered by our beliefs, values, and assumptions.

The language and behaviors which result from this can be useful or harmful. The expert NLP practitioner can help you model your behavior in a way which achieves your aims. For example, an NLP expert can help you model your behavior in a successful area of your life in areas where you feel you need some help.

Neuro Linguistic Programming is a discipline which is used for a huge variety of human behavior, from improving work performance to developing strategic thinking through to therapy. It is important, therefore that you choose a practitioner who works in the areas which you want to address.

Many modern hypnotherapists are also trained in neuro linguistic programming, as I am myself. So, finding a properly trained and registered hypnotherapist who also has these extra skills is probably the best route if you want help with emotional or behavioral issues.

Emotional Freedom Technique

Emotional Freedom Technique is a tool for healing emotional pain by tapping on the energy, or meridian points on the body. EFT works to restore balance to the body's energy and by doing so builds wellbeing and overcomes negative emotion. By tapping on the meridian points, you can restore the balance.

The basic technique is simple, you focus on your negative emotion, or what is upsetting you. Tap on each of the points while accepting yourself and committing to resolve the negative state and the balance of energy will soon be restored.

Gary has now retired, and there are many different organizations which both offer and teach EFT techniques. As with NLP, many hypnotherapists are trained in and use EFT. I would recommend that you choose a well-qualified and trained hypnotherapist who also has the skills in EFT.

A Quick Favor Please?

If this book helped you in any way, then may I ask you for a quick favor?

Would you please leave an honest review on Amazon?

Reviews are essential for authors, as they bring these simple but powerfully healing books to the awareness of more people. My mission is simply to help as many people as I can, and you can be a part of bringing that love and joy simply by leaving a review.

In Thanks,

Hena Husain